Good to
Excelente

Also by Bradley Hartmann

Spanish Twins
*Start Speaking Spanish on the Construction
Site with Words You Already Know*

Safety Spanish
Simple Spanish Skills for Solving Safety Problems

Behind Your Back
*What Purchasing Managers Say Once You Leave
the Room and How to Get Them to Say Yes*

Construction ESL
*Building Confidence on the Job Site with English
Language Skills*

Good to Excelente

How Excellent Companies Embrace
Hispanic Cultural Differences to Improve
Productivity, Safety, Retention, and Sales

Bradley Hartmann

RED ANGLE

A NEW PERSPECTIVE ON LANGUAGE AND LEADERSHIP

Good to excelente: how excellent companies embrace
Hispanic cultural differences to improve productivity,
safety, retention, and sales / Bradley Hartmann

ISBN: 978-1-7348220-1-4
Printed in the United States of America.

redangleinc.com

 2 3 4 5 6 7 8 9 10

SECOND EDITION

Cover design by Niche Labs
nichelabs.com

Formatting by NuLogic Creative
nulogiccreative.com

To my parents, Scott and Joyce Hartmann,
for always encouraging me to be *excelente*.

CONTENTS

CONTENTS

Context

"When Donald Trump is elected president, none of this shit will matter anymore."

It was the summer of 2015, just days after Donald Trump had announced his candidacy for president of the United States. The Republican candidate's speaking points included closing borders and building walls. This was the speech where Trump informed his audience that Mexico was not sending its best people across the border. No, he said, Mexico was sending drug dealers and rapists. Adding, "And some, I assume, are good people."

The aforementioned *shit* in question was the training content I was delivering at an interactive, half-day workshop. The training included construction-specific Spanish-language skills and cultural awareness concepts designed to help managers improve their communication efforts with their largely Spanish-speaking workforce—while also teaching how Hispanic cultures are different from the culture of the United States. I was at this particular construction site for two reasons: employee retention and safety.

The company's workforce, overwhelmingly Hispanic, was turning over nearly 100 percent each year. Before they left for another employer, however, Hispanics were getting injured. Often. More than $2 million had been spent on workers-comp claims the previous year alone.

Business needs aside, comments like the one above are an occupational hazard in my line of work. The middle-aged superintendent from Oklahoma who uttered it was not happy about being told to learn Spanish or how to build trust among Hispanics.

"OK. Why won't it matter anymore?" I asked, genuinely curious.

"Cuz once Trump is in the White House, he'll deport all the Mexicans."

"You mean, Trump promised to deport the 11 million undocumented immigrants in the U.S.," I clarified.

"Yes. That's what I mean. Thank you," he said with a chuckle, appreciating my amendment.

"OK, say Trump is elected," I began, "and he deports 11 million undocumented immigrants. Do you think our current labor shortage in the industry will worsen?" The superintendent agreed this was plausible.

"As a manager, then, with a short supply of talented craft workers," I continued, "won't it be even more important to keep the best Hispanic workers that *do* work for you?"

"Maybe, but I don't really care. If they don't speak English and don't assimilate to American culture, they need to go."

Having only moments earlier discussed the kinds of biases and prejudices that can have a negative impact on leadership capabilities, I asked, "Do you think the Hispanic workers under your supervision feel this cultural bias now?"

"Of course. I make sure they do. It's who I am and what I believe."

It's been nearly two years since my conversation with this superintendent. I've thought about him often, curious if he's changed his behavior—one way or another —now that Donald J. Trump has indeed become the 45th president of these United States.

Regardless of whom you voted for in the 2016 presidential election or how you feel about the results, glance around at the people near you. We are more similar than we are different. And now—as we've always done as a nation—we must move forward together, in some ways imperfect but improving every day.

How we choose to treat one another—be it the Russian mason, the Irish operator, the Hispanic welder, the African-American electrician, or the white guy sitting in the cube next to you—will always matter.

And nearly all, you can assume, are good people.

Thank you for reading.

Bradley Hartmann
February 2017
Dallas, Texas

*. . . the most obvious, important realities
are often the ones that are hardest to see
and talk about.*

—David Foster Wallace

Introducción

THE EXECUTIVE MADE A BEELINE TOWARD ME following my
presentation at a construction education conference in
2015. Striding up to me at the podium, he skipped the
traditional niceties.

No greeting.
No introduction.

"Look," he said, cutting to the chase, "we've got hundreds
of leadership classes for the managers in our organization, and not one has to do with preparing them to lead
Hispanic workers—even though they make up the overwhelming majority of our workforce."

I told him his company was certainly not alone.

"So, here's my question to you." His index finger shot out
like a switchblade, inches from my chest. "If the leaders in
my company can't communicate with their workforce and
don't understand how to change their workers' behaviors,
what do they need to know, and how quickly can we train
them up?"

The question was simple. The answer—a bit harder to
articulate. I started by describing my company, Red
Angle, our niche in the industry, and what it is we do.
Then I stopped midway through, took a deep breath, and
repeated the question back to the exec.

"What do they need to know, and how quickly can we
train them up?"

The executive nodded and peered at me expectantly.

"What do they need to know?"
What you hold in your hands now (a couple years too late
for this particular executive, I'm afraid) is the answer to
that question. *Good to Excelente* distills the fundamental

lessons from Red Angle's collaboration with more than one hundred companies and our training of thousands of employees across the country.

The two broad answers to this question comprise the two parts of *Good to Excelente*: culture and language.

Culture has been called the "software of the mind" by Geert Hofstede, the Dutch social psychologist and founding father of cultural intelligence inside the organization. In Part I, I will dissect the most relevant segments of his research to improve your ability to persuade, influence, and establish trust with your Hispanic workforce.

The second part of *Good to Excelente* is focused on language.

Learning a foreign language can be tricky. And given the lack of funding these days to language programs in this country's school systems, the language landscape for our children is looking starker and starker. Even in schools where foreign languages are still taught, proficiency isn't a guarantee.

"I took three years of high school Spanish and other than swear words, *cerveza*, and *baño*, I can't speak a lick."

I hear variations of this statement so often I now begin my *Construction Spanish* workshops by asking for a show of hands to whom it applies.

But fear not!

Having majored in Spanish in college, spent some time living in Mexico, and connected with Spanish speakers on the job for the last 25 years, I can tell you personally that learning basic, relevant Spanish skills that you can apply immediately isn't nearly as difficult as you might think.

I'll show you the fastest path to speaking relevant Spanish on the job.

"How quickly can we train them up?"
The philosophy at the heart of *Good to Excelente* centers around a concept called the **M**inimum **E**ffective **D**ose (MED). The term was originally conceived by Nautilus founder Arthur Jones, but I first learned of the MED from Tim Ferriss, author and self-described human guinea pig, who adopts the concept of the MED in his book *The 4-Hour Body*.

Through his books, podcast, and television show, Ferriss is in constant pursuit of achieving maximum results with the smallest amount of effort possible.

THE MINIMUM EFFECTIVE DOSE
The smallest dose that will produce a desired result. It's not laziness; it's focusing on what you want to achieve and then executing a plan to produce that result as efficiently as possible.

From speaking with high achievers about the MED, I've learned that many initially recoil at its definition.

"What?" they exclaim. "The smallest amount of effort possible? That sounds more like laziness. Not to mention it contradicts the lectures I give to my ten-year-old about learning long division!"

I know.

Frame it this way: the MED is the smallest dose that will produce a desired result. Anything beyond the MED is wasteful and redundant.

The analogy Ferriss uses is boiling water. Water boils at 212°F, plain and simple. After that, adding any more heat

or extending the time after boiling is unnecessary. You
have already achieved the desired result: boiling water.

Congrats, now go do something else with your time,
energy, and focus.

The same idea applies here. The goal of *Good to Excelente*
(G2E) is to get you trained up as quickly as possible and
with only the most necessary information and insights
required to deliver the desired results—helping you
become a better leader to everyone on your job, regardless
of cultural background or language preference.

The diagram below illustrates the G2E Leadership
Framework. Your ability to lead is shaped by two things:
what you say and what you do. That's it.

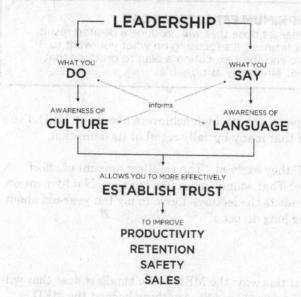

Your awareness of culture will drive your leadership
behavior (what you do). Your awareness of language will
drive what you say. However, culture will inform what
you say and language will inform what you do.

When combined, you will be able to more effectively establish trust—the foundation of leadership and meaningful relationships. Once you've established trust, achieving your goals of productivity, retention, safety, and sales (or any combination of these) becomes more realistic.

Only after you've established trust can you begin to think about going from good to great to *excelente*.

Good to great to *excelente*
Flywheels.
Hedgehogs.
Doom Loops.
Level 5 Leaders.

And a lot of metaphors involving people, buses, and seats.

Good to Great, by Jim Collins, is one of the best-selling business books of all time. Listing above just a few of the catch phrases from the book instantly teleports me back to 2002, just after the book had come out. After reading Collins's instant classic, I, like many people, was hooked—so much so that a co-worker of mine would tally the number of times I would reference it during meetings. The ratio typically hovered near 1:5—one *Good to Great* reference for every five minutes of meeting time.

And why not?

Every company wanted to learn the secrets of making the leap from good to great. The book delivered memorable stories and a common language for framing leadership and managerial challenges.

Good to Great is a book about the past
Jim Collins already had the answers to the test. Before he even set out to write his book, he started with a simple question: "Which companies have been the most profitable over the past 30 years." With this premise in hand, his

team began reading articles, press releases, and 10-Q reports and then interviewed scores of executives, collecting anecdotes and advice about what these companies *had done* to become so great.

Good to Excelente is a book about the future

Organizations across the country are struggling to adapt to an increasingly Hispanic workforce and grappling with what that means for the allocation of the Holy Trinity of corporate resources: capital, talent, and time.

The future will increasingly be described as *el futuro*. Spanish will increasingly be the language of preference on the job. And behavior will increasingly be rooted in cultural dimensions different from our own "American" culture.

The *excelente* companies of tomorrow will be the organizations that understand the growing Hispanic workforce and learn how to attract, hire, train, and retain it consistently.

Different cultures see the world differently.
Hispanic cultures are no exception.

Hispanic cultures raise their children differently, form ideas differently, teach differently in schools, and interact with authority differently. All these differences have an impact on Hispanics' behavior in the workplace and on your ability to lead.

As we will discuss in Chapter 1, many companies have *recognized* the large and growing Hispanic workforce. To become *excelente*, though, your organization will need to *accept* this truth as well—and then act upon it.

WAIT.

We're in America, right?
In America, we speak English.

We're the most immigrant-friendly country in the world.
All we ask is that, once here, immigrants assimilate, just
like our ancestors did when they first arrived here.

Right?

Well . . .

Regardless of where you stand on this issue personally,
from a business perspective, this misses the point. After
all, let's not forget why you're here: productivity, safety,
retention, sales. You're running a business, not a country.
But! The politics of immigrant employees and the related
cultural barriers no doubt present in your workforce still
play a part in all this.

The point of this book is to help you learn more about
your Hispanic workforce and their culture and language.
Because the more you *know* about them, the better
equipped you'll be at effectively *managing* them. And the
better you are at that, the better your business will be. So
set aside your personal thoughts on patriotism and focus
on the brass tacks at hand: capitalism.

Be a capitalist
Back in 2012, I was finalizing a Red Angle contract. A
trio of successful pilot programs and the green light from
multiple layers of management had landed me in the
CEO's office of a billion-dollar construction firm.

The pen was in his hand, literally on the dotted line.
"Before I sign this," he said slowly, "I gotta ask. Are you a
Democrat?"

Caught off guard by the non sequitur (at no point in the

courtship-to-partnership process had anyone in the
company discussed politics), I feigned a hearing problem.

"I'm sorry, sir. Can you repeat that?"

"C'mon!" he roared, with an air of mischief in his voice.
"You're from Chicago! You're a white guy helping people
speak Spanish to Mexicans! Of course you're a Democrat!
I got a few questions for you, then . . ."

One quick glance around the table at his lieutenants told
me there was no cavalry coming to my rescue.

"Seriously. You're a Democrat, aren't you?" he asked
again. He seemed like he actually wanted to talk about
this. Now.

Of all the scenarios I'd planned for to seal this deal, this
was not one of them. I decided to put my thumbs together
and go all in on this hand.

"If you want to talk politics, let's go grab a drink and chat.
But this isn't a political issue we're dealing with—it's
financial. You spent several million dollars last year in
workers' comp claims, 85 percent of which were injuries to
Hispanics. Three workers have died on your jobs in the
last 18 months. All three were Hispanic. Your executive
team estimates your annual rework north of $10 million,
and field management tells me communication is a
constant frustration. You employ a few hundred foreign-
born Hispanic craft workers, yet none of your training is
in Spanish . . ."

I paused, catching my breath.
The CEO's gaze was steady, betraying nothing.

To hell with it, I thought. I might as well finish my little
speech with a flourish.

"So, am I a Democrat? I'm a *capitalist*—just like you. We can help you and your team keep your hard-earned money, unless you enjoy doing all this for practice. With all due respect, I'd rather get to work than talk politics." The CEO stared at me.
The rest of the table stared at him.
"Fine then," he said abruptly.

He looked down, swirled his signature illegibly on the contract, and got up and left. He didn't utter a word to anyone on his way out.

Choose profitability over politics
This book is not for everyone.
That's OK.

I'm not for everyone, and neither are you.

This isn't a political debate.
It's far more practical.

The value of your business is the sum of its future earnings. And your future earnings are directly tied to those who perform the work. Now and—increasingly—in the future, the Hispanic workforce will drive your profitability.

We've got work to do and we can only get it done working together. Jack Welch, the legendary CEO of General Electric, called *candor* the biggest secret in business. Neither you nor I have the time to tiptoe around sensitive topics or muddle through the morass of political correctness.

If your workforce is Hispanic, you have a choice to make: profitability or politics?

If you struggle separating the politics involved from the practicality of working together with the Hispanic workforce, I recommend you close this book now and read something else.

Life is too short.

Focus on something else.

Because sometimes the hardest things to see are right in front of us.

Recognition without acceptance
"We do cultural-intelligence training all the time."

This statement surprised me. Although I've discussed with dozens of construction firms the concept of cultural intelligence—training employees to understand the differences among cultures and how those can affect leadership and management (in this book, we'll refer to this as one's "cultural IQ")—none included cultural IQ training as a standard discipline.

"That's great," I replied to the executive of a project I was working on, impressed. "Tell me more about it."

"Sure," he said. "We're a global company, so when we construct a liquefied natural gas plant in Indonesia and we send someone from, say, Atlanta, we need to equip that employee with the cultural skills to lead intelligently. What we do *here* won't necessarily work *there*."

I admitted my lack of experience building Indonesian liquefied natural gas plants and then asked, "So, what kind of training is involved prior to making one of your employees an expat?"[1]

"There are full-day workshops that include role playing and activities that help you to think differently, to see the world through a different lens. It's important because when you manage workers from a different culture, you need to understand the context from their perspective, including some of the history, basic geography, their beliefs, their values, customs—all that stuff is important."

"Do you conduct cultural IQ training for all cultures where you work?" I asked, trying to understand the scope of their training.

"Pretty much. If we have a job where the workforce is culturally different, we need to be sensitive to that and prepare our teams for it."

I agreed. "Given the billions of dollars' worth of jobs you have here in the United States, have you been through cultural IQ training for Hispanic cultures?"

He paused. I heard a brief, forced exhale through the phone.

"You mean. . . Spanish? Projects in Spain?" he asked, his voice rising a few octaves.

"No, I mean projects in the U.S. built largely by workers from Mexico or Guatemala or Puerto Rico or the Dominican Republic," I said.

Silence.

I continued, "There's a large percentage of Hispanic craft workers on your jobs here in the U.S., right?"

"Oh, geez," the executive began. "Yeah. Probably 90 percent. Or more."

"I would guess that with cultural IQ training being so common, it would be done on jobs where 90 percent of the workforce is culturally different. Hispanics are culturally different, right? With a different perspective on history. With different beliefs, values, and all that important stuff."

There was irritation in the executive's voice. "Sure, but we're in America. We don't need to do cultural IQ training for jobs here in the United States."

"Why not?" I asked. "Well, to be honest, that's their problem. Not ours."

Whether you are building in Indonesia or Indianapolis, your ability to connect, persuade, influence, and ultimately solve problems with the workers on the job will determine your success.

The workforce is changing.
Culturally, it is increasingly Hispanic.[2]
Linguistically, it is increasingly Spanish.[3]

These changes are happening on your job—and it's up to *you* to address them. Or rather, it's your opportunity to become *excelente*.

The G2E Leadership Framework
This book is broken down into two parts—culture and language. Each part has three chapters.

GOOD TO *EXCELENTE* FRAMEWORK™

AWARENESS OF CULTURE

| RECOGNIZE + ACCEPT LA REALIDAD | UNDERSTAND THE ORIGINS | DISTINGUISH AMONG THE DIMENSIONS |

AWARENESS OF LANGUAGE

| SECRET OF THE SPANISH TWINS | EMBRACE THE EQUATION | FORWARD WITH (MICRO) FLUENCY |

As you can see in the diagram above, the arrows on the far left and far right are two-sided. Culture affects language and vice versa.

Part I is designed to help upgrade your cultural IQ quickly.

But why address culture first? Good question.
We will address culture first because you can still become an effective leader of Hispanic employees without any actual Spanish-language skills—Red Angle has helped executive teams do just this by ensuring that a coherent strategy focused on Hispanic workers and in accordance with Hispanic cultures is in place for their business.

For example, efforts to attract, hire, train, and retain the best available craft workers should take into account cultural background.

As you'll see throughout this book, individuals from different places think differently. Intuitively, we know this, yet few companies carry this understanding through to their operational decision making. In marketing, we would develop different "buyer personas" for each segment of the potential customer base. Small adjustments would be made in messaging, placement, or delivery method based on the customers' cultural preferences.

The same concept applies here. If you don't have the right cultural IQ, you won't be able to effectively manage and lead a culturally diverse workforce.

From my experience at Red Angle and from working with hundreds of executives, I often witness leaders having *aha* moments where operational observations of the Hispanic workforce are coupled with insights about Hispanic cultures. When this happens, operational adjustments seem obvious only in retrospect.

Two parts, six chapters
In Chapter 1, *Recognize and Accept La Realidad*, we provide insights and dispel myths around our current reality—*la realidad*—to ensure we begin from a solid foundation of facts.

In Chapter 2, *Understand the Origins*, we walk through a brief tour of the top five most populated Hispanic countries of origin (or commonwealths, as we address Puerto Rico) to gain a better understanding of how history and geography have shaped their cultures, including a closer look at each country through five specific lenses: people, places, events, concepts, and food.

In Chapter 3, *Distinguish Among the Dimensions*, we introduce the pioneers of cultural intelligence and highlight the most fundamental cultural dimensions that apply to being able to lead Hispanic workers on the job effectively.

Part II focuses on language-learning strategies and tactics not taught in schools to help you speak and understand Spanish on the job.

In Chapter 4, *The Secret of the Spanish Twins*, we reveal the fastest way to acquire new words and phrases that are relevant to your business.

In Chapter 5, *Embrace the Equation*, we break down the three language-training factors that, if practiced, guarantee language retention.

Lastly, in Chapter 6, *Forward with (micro) Fluency*, we discuss small steps you can take to move toward job-specific Spanish fluency.

Now that we've outlined the six chapters of the book—what's at stake?

Improve productivity
Cultural and language barriers often introduce potential ambiguity at work, which can inhibit productivity. The goal of every job is to do it right the first time. However, when culture and language differences enter the equation, a lot can get lost in translation, preventing you from getting something right.

It's like the game Telephone: one person creates an original sentence and shares it with the person next to him,
who listens and then repeats it to the person next to her,
and so on until it gets to the final person, who inevitably
hears something completely different from what the first
person said. In a children's game, it can be amusing. On
the job, it can be frustrating, inefficient, and potentially
dangerous.

As we dig deep into the cultural dimensions, you will
learn specific tactics and techniques to ensure work is
done right the first time. Most importantly, we will reveal
how cultures differ in terms of trust.

It is often said that among speed, quality, and price, you
can only pick two. That is only true when there is a bias
toward distrust. In high-trust relationships, you can
achieve—and come to expect—all three. Think of your
best customers. For them, you bend over backward to
deliver speed, quality, *and* price.

However, trust must be earned.

Improve safety
Hispanics are disproportionately
more likely to be injured or killed
while on the job. The
Occupational Safety and Health
Administration (OSHA) has made
Hispanic outreach a national
focus. OSHA notes:

*While overall workplace fatalities have dropped 20 percent
in the last decade, workplace fatalities among Hispanic
workers, especially those working in the construction
industry, have risen almost 35 percent in the same period.
As the industry attracts new, inexperienced workers,
often hired by second-, third-, or fourth-tier
subcontractors, Hispanic injuries and deaths will rise.*

Increase retention
People don't quit their jobs—they quit their leadership. If you are facing labor shortages now, just wait. It will get worse before it gets better. Yes, you will want to search for new talent, but start by differentiating your company to ensure your best workers don't leave.

Increase sales
Despite their immense and growing numbers, Hispanic customers[4] are often overlooked and misunderstood. As we'll discuss in Chapter 3, a hallmark of the Hispanic culture is its collectivist nature and family focus.

Family is a relative term (pun intended) among Hispanics. Family refers to an extended version that includes cousins, second cousins, friends, and friends of friends. Word-of-mouth referrals are extremely persuasive in Hispanic cultures. As a result, word-of-mouth is also the strongest—and the cheapest—form of marketing.

Additionally, as the 2016 Kauffman Index of Entrepreneurial Activity Noted:

> *Reflecting the longer-term trends showing rising Latino rates of entrepreneurship and a growing share of the total U.S. population, the Latino share of all new entrepreneurs rose from 10 percent in 1996 to 21 percent in 2015.*[5]

Good to *Excelente* leadership model redux
Leadership can be distilled down to two activities: what managers *do* and what managers *say*. That's it.

Culture is a collection of habits. Although your team may be *managing things*, without understanding these habits, they're not *leading people*.

Now, let's begin the process of improving from good to *excelente*.

1

Recognize and
Accept La Realidad

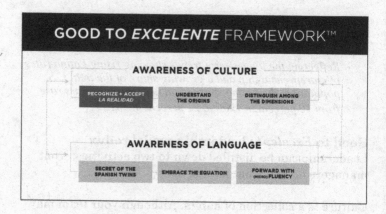

GOOD TO *EXCELENTE* FRAMEWORK™

AWARENESS OF CULTURE

| RECOGNIZE + ACCEPT LA REALIDAD | UNDERSTAND THE ORIGINS | DISTINGUISH AMONG THE DIMENSIONS |

AWARENESS OF LANGUAGE

| SECRET OF THE SPANISH TWINS | EMBRACE THE EQUATION | FORWARD WITH (MICRO) FLUENCY |

. . . the future depends on man's being able to transcend the limits of individual cultures. To do so, however, he must first recognize and accept the multiple hidden dimensions of unconscious culture, because every culture has its own hidden, unique form of unconscious culture.

—Edward T. Hall,
   Beyond Culture

RECOGNIZE AND ACCEPT *LA REALIDAD*

FROM MY COLLABORATION WITH RED ANGLE CLIENTS across the country and from helping them with their efforts to attract, hire, train, and retain Hispanic workers more effectively, one thing has remained clear: nearly everyone is aware of the value of the Hispanic workforce. Recognition, it seems, is not the issue.

Yes, they'll say, Hispanics are a critical component of the workforce. And yes, in the future, there will be more Hispanics on our jobs, not fewer. And, oh yes! Hispanics are indeed hardworking.

And yes, there is currently a labor shortage, and we need all the talent we can get. And of course, clear communication is critical on the job.

I hear this same feedback—on occasion begrudgingly, but most often candid, devoid of emotion—everywhere I go, from Seattle to Chicago to San Antonio to Charlotte.

I often recap the conversation for clarity. "So, there are a lot of Hispanics, and they are hardworking, growing in number, and essential to our business. Is that accurate?"

Heads nod. No, recognition is indeed not the issue. From the C-suite to the jobsite, many have *recognized* the reality—*la realidad*—of the growing Hispanic workforce and demographic but are slow to *accept* it. Doing so is a necessary step toward embracing Hispanic cultural differences as a competitive advantage.

While we have thousands of crumbling bridges across the nation, we talk about building walls along our southern border.

While we have a national labor shortage, we talk about deporting millions of Hispanics—the very people who represent (at least part of) the solution. The more we listen to—and buy into—the divisive political commentary dominating the news, the clarity of our reality diminishes. We stop trusting our own eyes and ears. We discount the diverse collaboration we see on our jobs every day.

We opt for the punch line instead of logic.
We outsource our thinking.

Accepting our reality begins with a few facts. In this chapter, we will review ten fundamental facts about where we stand today. Surely there are more details worth knowing, but consistent with our philosophy of the MED—the minimum effective dose—these quick shots of vital information will provide an effective baseline of knowledge from which to improve your leadership and understanding of the Hispanic workforce.

So, what does Hispanic actually mean? (And while we're at it, Latino.)

First things first: *Spanish* is a language. *Hispanic* is an adjective describing individuals with some ancestral connection to Spain.

All too often, I hear well-meaning people refer to "Hispanic speakers." I've learned to control my impulse to interrupt the speaker immediately and lecture them on the difference between the two... *Many Hispanics— but not all—are Spanish speakers. See the difference there, sir?*

It's a conversation killer, let me tell you.

Help me spread the word.

What about *Latino*?

During a cultural IQ workshop in New Jersey last year, I asked a Hispanic employee which term she preferred—*Hispanic* or *Latina*.

"I find the term Hispanic offensive," she said with disgust. "It's a word the government made up to group Mexicans, Puerto Ricans, Guatemalans, and other Spanish speakers into the same bucket to make it easier on them."

That is absolutely true.

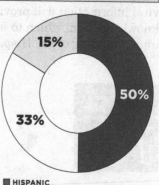

Hispanic or Latino?

15%

50%

33%

■ HISPANIC
□ LATINO
□ NO PREFERENCE

The term *Hispanic* officially arrived in the mid-1970s[1] as bureaucrats in Washington were trying to understand how many, well, Hispanics, lived in the country. The committee needed a catch-all term in lieu of "Spanish speakers," because, after all, many Hispanics living in the United States do not speak Spanish; many are quite fluent in English.

The committee determined that both *Hispanic* and *Latino* were acceptable, if not flawed, synonyms for individuals of Spanish and Latin American descent, respectively.

So . . . what should I say?

Research conducted by the Pew Research Center revealed that Hispanics do not overwhelmingly favor one over the other. But among those *who do have a preference*, *Hispanic* is preferred over *Latino* 2:1.[2]

How do Hispanics and Latinos self-identify? Hispanics identify with their country of origin. For example, ask someone from Honduras to identify between *Hispanic*, *Latino*, or *Honduran*, and they will overwhelmingly prefer *Honduran*. That is, after all, the country they came from.

For a Puerto Rican, given the option between *Hispanic*, *Latino*, or *Puerto Rican*, they will overwhelmingly prefer *Puerto Rican*.

You get the idea.

Having had this discussion for years now, I've learned it's better simply to ask individuals which designation they prefer. When they answer, ask them why, then use that terminology.

Which countries are Hispanic?
Hispanic and *Latino* generally refer to the following 20 locations ancestral to Spain:

North America (1)		
Mexico[3]		
Central America (7)		
Guatemala	*Nicaragua*	*Honduras*
Belize	*Costa Rica*	
El Salvador	*Panama*	
South America (9)		
Colombia	*Peru*	*Argentina*
Venezuela	*Bolivia*	*Paraguay*
Ecuador	*Chile*	*Uruguay*
Islands (3)		
Puerto Rico	*Cuba*	*The Dominican Republic*

In short, this list comprises Mexico and all the countries in Central and South America, with the exception of Brazil (they were under the Portuguese empire, hence the Portuguese spoken there), Haiti (French) and those three South American countries you always forget during games of *Trivial Pursuit*: Guyana, Suriname, and French Guiana.

Spanish-Speaking Countries Near You

How many Hispanics are there?

As of February 2017, there were 57 million Hispanics living in the United States.[4] With the total U.S. population at around 320 million, Hispanics represent about 18 percent.

U.S. Hispanic population	57M		U.S. Hispanic population, %	18%

COUNTRY / TERRITORY	% OF TOTAL	SIZE IN U.S.	% U.S. BORN	% FOREIGN BORN
MEXICO	64%	35.4M	67%	33%
PUERTO RICO	9.6%	5.3M	98%	2%
EL SALVADOR	3.8%	2.1M	41%	59%
CUBA	3.7%	2.0M	43%	57%
DOMINICAN REPUBLIC	3.2%	1.7M	46%	54%
GUATEMALA	2.4%	1.3M	37%	63%
COLOMBIA	1.9%	1.0M	36%	64%
HONDURAS	1.5%	0.8M	39%	61%
SPAIN	1.4%	0.75M	85%	15%
ECUADOR	1.2%	0.7M	39%	61%

Source: U.S. Census Bureau

If you must guess . . .

Mexican and Puerto Rican heritage (64 percent and 10 percent, respectively) represent three out of every four Hispanics in the United States. In Chapter 5, we'll introduce a simple script to help you ask Spanish speakers where they are from. We'll play the odds here and prepare you for the two most common responses: Mexico and Puerto Rico.

Born in the U.S.A.
Note from the chart (page 29) that 33 percent of Mexicans are foreign born. That means 67 percent of Mexicans in the United States *were born here*. Many Red Angle workshop participants are surprised by this statistic, suggesting the figure should be flipped.

Are you sure? Two out of every three Mexicans were born in Mexico and came to the United States illegally, right? Wrong.

When you hear people throw around the phrase, "Go back to where you came from!" let them know that for two-thirds of Hispanics of Mexican descent, that is more likely to be across the street than across the border.

Not born in the U.S.A.
Other than Mexicans (33 percent), Puerto Ricans (2 percent), and Spaniards (15 percent), the other seven countries of origin are more than half foreign born. Throughout the following chapters, we will stress the importance of understanding what percentage of the general Hispanic workforce in the U.S. is foreign born.

For these individuals, we will have to develop systems and processes to better understand their language preference, as well as their ability to read and write Spanish or English.

Specific to safety on the job, foreign-born workers often have years of reinforced behavior in their native country that frames their idea of *safety*. Few have safety standards on par with those in the United States, which is partly the reason why Hispanics are disproportionately more likely to be injured or killed on the job. (More on that in Chapter 3.)

3 TRES

They're not all Mexicans.

While speaking to a construction-management class at a Midwestern university last year, I asked the class if anyone experienced language and/or cultural barriers on the job. One student raised his hand immediately.

"For sure," he began. "Last summer, I interned at a concrete construction company, and all the workers were Mexicans. I was one of the few white guys out there."

"How do you know they were all from Mexico?" I asked.

The student gave me a confused look. "Um, whaddya mean?"

"You said 'all the workers were Mexican,'" I repeated for clarification. "I'm just curious how you knew they were all from Mexico, instead of, say, Puerto Rico or Guatemala."

"Oh, I see what you're saying," the student said, relieved.

"I guess I don't really know. If they had dark skin and spoke Spanish, we called them all Mexicans. Is that. . . no good?"

That is, to be sure, *no bueno*.

Want to piss off a Mexican?
Call him a Guatemalan.
And vice versa.

Want a Salvadoran to see red?
Call him Honduran.

And vice versa.

For those looking to increase their ability to lead and develop trust with their Hispanic workforce, this common misunderstanding is the easiest way to lose credibility and respect.

Yes, nearly 65 percent of all Hispanics in the United States are from Mexico. But while I'm not that good at math (I majored in Spanish for a reason), I'm fairly certain 65 percent does not equal 100 percent.

You may know this intuitively, but to be clear: it is not recommended to refer to any dark-skinned Spanish speaker as a Mexican. This is an ignorant mental shortcut.

Although the odds are in your favor, it is more prudent simply to ask people where they are from—¿De dónde eres?—which we will cover in more detail in Chapter 5.

4 CUATRO

Everybody is all-American.

We Americans are a patriotic bunch. We tend to believe we are the best at pretty much everything (often objectively true, thanks to people like Michael Phelps). As such, many believe that the world should conform to us.

Americans rule.
And Americans speak English.

Except, no. . . that is false.
Most Americans actually speak Spanish.

We "Americans" (U.S.A.! U.S.A.!) often forget about those beyond our borders. In fact, there are multiple Americas: North America (including Mexico), Central America, and South America.

It might surprise you to know that these people also refer to themselves as "Americans."

Back in 2016, I had the pleasure of meeting an employee of a client I was working with at the time, Ana-María Phillips. After talking with Ana-María and learning about some of her backstory, I realized she has a unique perspective on this "American" designation. The daughter of Welsh/Italian and Guatemalan parents, Ana-María was born in Panama. Her father was in the military and was later reassigned to Paraguay for several years before returning to Biloxi, Mississippi. In the truest sense of the term, Ana-María is *American*.

Today, Ana-María lives in San Antonio. Having lived extensively in North, Central, and South America, she was sensitive to my narrow usage of the term *Americans*.

Fulfilling the stereotype, I had real difficulty not calling Americans *Americans* during my Red Angle cultural IQ workshops.

In subsequent workshops, I tried exchanging *Americans* for *Citizens of the U.S.*, but the three extra syllables proved too large a hurdle for me.

As a guest on my podcast, *Red Angle Radio*, I asked Ana-María to expound on her American sensibility.

> *We're all* Americans. *If we come from Central or South or North America, we're all Americans. And so, the idea of using the term* American *to describe someone from the U.S. only. . . to be honest, doesn't sit well with me, because we're all Americans. And you hear people throughout Latin America and South America say* Todos somos Americanos—*We're all Americans. So, it's just typical, I think, of the U.S. mind-set to be very ethnocentric, to say, "We're the Americans." Well. . . no.*

Ana-María is right. While we *Americans* from the United States are aware of the three Americas (North, Central, and South), we simply don't think in those terms. But we should.

To lock in an image with this concept, I use the team logo of the *Club de Fútbol América*.

As for Club America's mascot? It is the Águilas (the Eagles).

Based in Mexico City, Club América is the New England Patriots of fútbol—arguably the most successful club in the Mexican league.

And they are often referred to simply as *América*.

Todos somos Americanos.
We're all Americans.

5 CINCO

"Hispanic Smile" no más.

In the 1980s, Hispanics resided in what I've heard some people refer to as the "Hispanic Smile." At the time, Hispanics predominantly lived in California, Arizona, New Mexico, Texas, Florida, and New York, inhabiting a curved stretch of land from coast to coast that resembled a smile.

Mainland U.S.A. was the face.
Hispanics lived in the smile.
Hence, the Hispanic Smile.

(Note: For the record, there were also 1 million Hispanics living in Chicago at the time, but that ruined the "smile" metaphor, so it was ignored.)

For a time, this was accurate.
Not so much anymore.

While those *smiley* states still maintain large Hispanic populations, look at the states with the highest rates of Hispanic growth since 2000:

	STATE	% GROWTH SINCE 2000
1	ALABAMA	158%
2	SOUTH CAROLINA	154%
3	TENNESSEE	154%
4	KENTUCKY	132%
5	SOUTH DAKOTA	129%
6	ARKANSAS	123%
7	NORTH CAROLINA	120%
8	MISSISSIPPI	117%
9	MARYLAND	112%
10	GEORGIA	103%

TOP 10

U.S. States
with
Fastest-Growing
Hispanic Populations,
2000-14

Source: U.S. Census Bureau

If, like me, numbers presented in lists have a sedating effect on your brain, here is one key takeaway: Georgia, at number ten, experienced 103 percent growth in its Hispanic population between 2000 and 2014. This means the Hispanic population doubled in little more than a decade. The top three states—Alabama, South Carolina, and Tennessee—doubled as well. And they appear on their way to double yet again.

There is no Hispanic Smile any longer. Hispanics are growing in number in nearly every single state in the nation—including Alaska. Regardless of where you live and how much you employ, subcontract, or sell to Hispanics today, you (or your competition) will be doing more of it in the future.

The *Three Amigos* of *estadísticas*
As we think about the growth of the Hispanic demographic, we must understand three key data sets.

We just reviewed Hispanic population growth. This statistic, expressed as a percentage, indicated the rate of Hispanic population *growth*. The *total* number of Hispanics in the state may be large or small—the Hispanic growth rate evaluates the rate of change over time.

In addition to Hispanic growth, two other stats, or *estadísticas*, are critical to keep in mind. Below is a brief description of each along with the ten state leaders for the category.

Total population
Fairly straightforward concept here. The total population indicates the Hispanic headcount living in a specific state. California and Texas dominate, while Georgia appears at the #10 spot in both the fastest-growing and total-population lists.

	STATE	POP IN MILLIONS
1	CALIFORNIA	14.4
2	TEXAS	9.8
3	FLORIDA	4.4
4	NEW YORK	3.5
5	ILLINOIS	2.1
6	ARIZONA	1.9
7	NEW JERSEY	1.6
8	COLORADO	1.1
9	NEW MEXICO	1.0
10	GEORGIA	0.9

TOP 10
U.S. States
by Hispanic
Population
2014

Source: U.S. Census Bureau

Population percentage

Population percentage takes the total number of residents in a given state divided by the total number of Hispanics in the state.

	STATE	% HISPANIC
1	NEW MEXICO	46.7%
2	TEXAS	38.1%
3	CALIFORNIA	38.1%
4	ARIZONA	30.1%
5	NEVADA	27.1%
6	FLORIDA	22.8%
7	COLORADO	20.9%
8	NEW JERSEY	18.1%
9	NEW YORK	18.0%
10	ILLINOIS	16.1%

Source: U.S. Census Bureau

TOP 10
U.S. States
by Percentage
of Hispanic
Population
2014

This list is essentially a reshuffling of the total-population list from the previous page. This seems logical. The largest Hispanic populations in the United States constitute a large percentage of their state populations.

The one state not in the top ten of total Hispanic population but present in this list is Nevada, ranking #5 with a Hispanic population of more than 27 percent.

Bottom line: Regardless of whom you employ or to whom you sell, your team needs to think strategically about the growing Hispanic population in your state.

6 SEIS

Birth rate, not immigration.

Birth rate, not immigration, is driving Hispanic growth. Of all the divisive political rhetoric and fake news, this fact has been obscured the most.

Birth rate, not immigration, is driving Hispanic growth.

This is important since we, as American voters, influence the allocation of our precious national resources: which is to say, our capital, our attention, and our time. We may or may not choose to build a 2,000-mile wall along our border with Mexico, but we must be aware this will not materially affect the Hispanic population in the United States.

Why not?
Say it with me now: birth rate, not immigration, is driving Hispanic growth. The fertility rate—essentially the average number of children per woman—for the United States as a whole is 1.8.

Fertility Rates, by Race & Hispanic Origin, 2014

Fertility Rate

Non-Hispanic White · Non-Hispanic Black · Hispanic · Asian or Pacific Islander

Race/Ethnicity
■ Non-Hispanic White
□ Non-Hispanic Black
□ Hispanic
■ Asian or Pacific Isl...

Source: Hamilton, B.E., Martin, J.A., Osterman, M.J.K., Curtin, S.C., &Matthews, T.J. (2015). Births: Final data for 2014. National Vital Statistics Reports, 64(12). Hyattsville, MD: National Center for Health Statistics. Available at http://www.cdc.gov/nchs/data/nvsr/nvsr64/nvsr64_12.pdf. Table 5.

For Hispanics, that figure is 2.4—33 percent higher.

Before the Great Recession, the Hispanic fertility rate was 3.7, a small number that belies the Hispanic-population boom experienced in the 1990s and early 2000s.

Immigration did drive Hispanic growth for some time. In the '70s, '80s, and '90s, immigration outpaced birth rate as the primary driver of Hispanic growth. But not anymore.

For the last two decades, birth rate, not immigration, has driven Hispanic growth.

As for the future? Today, 25 percent of all babies born in the United States are Hispanic. As this trend continues, we can likely expect to see an increase from the current percentage of Hispanics in the United States, 18 percent (or around 57 million), to at least this much.

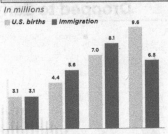

Sources of Hispanic Population Growth, by Decade

In millions

■ U.S. births ■ Immigration

Source: Data for 2000s based on Pew Research Center tabulations of 2000 Census (5% IPUMS) and 2010 American Community Survey (1% IPUMS). Data for 1970s, 1980s, and 1990s drawn from Pew Research Center historical projections (Passel and Cohn, 2008)

PEW RESEARCH CENTER

Uncle Sam: Net exporter of Mexicans

Furthermore, since 2009 more Mexicans have left the United States than have entered it. This is known as *negative net migration*. The current net migration stats between the United States and Mexico are at levels not seen since the 1940s.[5]

Sounds like liberal BS to me

I feel your skepticism, and I like it. We all need to hold one another—and ourselves—more accountable to the truth.

Is there another side to the story?

How can we fact check this birth rate–immigration theory?

Well, we have a federal agency that handles that: the Border Patrol.

According to U.S. Border Patrol data, the number of Mexican migrants caught at the border in 2015 was the lowest it's been in nearly 50 years.

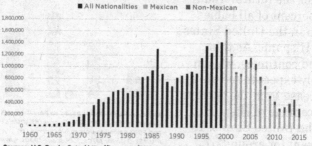

Southwest Border Apprehensions Have Dropped to Early 1970s Levels

■ All Nationalities ■ Mexican ■ Non-Mexican

Sources: U.S. Border Patrol http://1.usa.gov/1W4vtwR and http://1.usa.gov/1W4vuAR

7 SIETE

Boomers out, Hispanics in.

According to the Pew Research Center, ten thousand
Baby Boomers will turn 65 every day for the next 13
years. The size of the Boomer generation has significantly
increased the median age of the U.S. population as a
whole. Quick flashback to fifth-grade math, in case you
haven't had your morning coffee yet.

Median: the number in the middle of a data set.
Mean: the average.
Mode: don't worry about it; no one ever uses it.[6]

Great. Back to the point. The median age of the U.S.
population as a whole is 38. The median age of the white
population is 43.

And what is the
median age of
Hispanics? 28.

That means
Hispanics are nearly
25 percent younger
than the nation as a
whole. Mexicans,
who represent nearly
65 percent of all
Hispanics in the
country, are even
younger (26).

So what?
Good question.

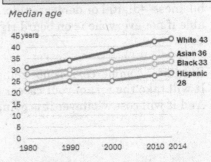

**Hispanics Are the Nation's
Youngest Major
Racial/Ethnic Group**

Median age

45 years — White 43
Asian 36
Black 33
Hispanic 28

1980   1990   2000   2010 2014

*Source: Pew Research Center analysis of 2010 and
2014 American Community Surveys and 1980, 1990
and 2000 decentennial censuses (IPUMS). "The
Nation's Latino Population Is Defined by Its Youth"*

PEW RESEARCH CENTER

Demography is destiny

If you work with or sell to Hispanics, any coherent strategy should include an acknowledgement of the demographic reality unfolding in these United States of America.

In January of 2013, *Fast Company* magazine published a story about Walmart's slow transition to digital retailing against Amazon.com.

Neil Ashe, president and CEO of global e-commerce at Walmart, encouraged the Bentonville faithful to think long term—not Wall Street long term, but decades long term.

> *"Somebody at one of the board meetings asked me, 'Neil, how long is this going to take, and how much is it going to cost?'" Ashe recalls. "And I said, 'It's going to take the rest of our careers, and it's going to cost whatever it costs. Because this isn't a project, this is the company.'"*[7]

The demographic change in America is like that.
It's a long-term commitment.

You cannot ignore the fundamental shifts affecting your business—digital or demographic. And it is understand-able if not everyone is on board right now. It will take time.

But like e-commerce, it is not going away.
It will take the rest of your career to continually adapt.
And it will cost whatever it is going to cost.

8 OCHO

Legal Eagles . . . and Águilas Ilegales.

How many Hispanics are living here illegally—or, better put—undocumented? Current estimates number around 11 million.

That is 20 percent of the total Hispanic population. So, an estimated two out of every ten Hispanics living in the United States are undocumented. Think of it as the 80/20 rule: 80 percent legal, 20 percent undocumented.

Although 11 million undocumented people living in the United States is a large number, it is still less than 3.5 percent of the total population. You can form your own opinion as to how alarming these numbers are, but it is critical we keep context in mind.

Some political discourse on the issue will leave undiscerning listeners under the impression that, indeed, the reverse is true—that 80 percent (not 20 percent) of all Hispanics are undocumented and that 35 percent (not 17 percent) of the total population is Hispanic.

At one point in time, illegal immigration was occurring at a high rate. Not so much now.

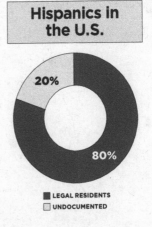

Hispanics in the U.S.

20%

80%

■ LEGAL RESIDENTS
□ UNDOCUMENTED

Think about it. When you look back on the Great Recession, other than employees at Bear Stearns and Lehman Brothers, who were some of the first to feel the initial sting? After the economy slammed on the brakes, construction activity halted as well, and manufacturing initiated its "reduction in force" (my personal favorite euphemism for "layoffs"). As a result, many Hispanics were the first to lose their jobs.

A lot of them then left the industry, the country, or both.

The seeds of our current labor shortage were sowed in the dark days following the economic collapse of 2006–07. And while the American economy has surged back to life since then, illegal immigration has not.

People are entitled to their own opinions, but not their own facts. Remember the 80/20 rule: 80 percent of Hispanics in this country are here legally.

9 NUEVE

The Américas: A great place to die.

In the spring and summer of 2014, you may recall the
United States had a legitimate crisis along our border
with Mexico. But this particular crisis was different from
our current situation in two regards. First, the vast majority of immigrants coming to the U.S. were not Mexican,
but rather Guatemalan, Salvadoran, and Honduran.

Second, these were children.
Roughly 57,000 of them.[8]

Only the most perilous of circumstances would ever force
parents to send unchaperoned children, most under the
age of 12, to travel more than 1,000 miles across three
countries in hopes of a safer destination. But for many
people in Central America, this is a reality.

*(Interesting aside regarding precedent: In the early 1960s, not
long after Fidel Castro had seized power in Cuba, the U.S.
government, in collaboration with the Catholic Church,
facilitated the safe relocation of 14,000 unaccompanied Cuban
children throughout the United States. We will delve a little more
into this historically relevant event—known as Operation Peter
Pan—in Chapter 2.)*

The Migration Policy Institute, an independent,
nonpartisan, nonprofit think tank in Washington, D.C.,
that tracks the movement of people globally, confirmed
the cause of this youth movement:

> *In particular, all three Northern Triangle countries
> [El Salvador, Guatemala, and Honduras] continue to
> experience high levels of violence, food insecurity,
> and poverty. . .* [9]

Many people in the United States are unaware of the extent of the violence and instability just across our southern border, particularly in Central America. Many of these countries, rife with violent gangs fueled by drug trafficking, are some of the most violent places on Earth. Among the top ten countries in the world with the highest murder rate per 100,000 people, four of them—Honduras, El Salvador, Belize, and Guatemala—are within 1,000 miles of the U.S. border.

With violence on such a scale, we cannot be surprised when parents are willing to risk the journey across Central America in hopes of safe harbor for their children.

	COUNTRY	MURDER RATE
1	HONDURAS	84.6
2	EL SALVADOR	64.2
3	VENEZUELA	62.0
4	VIRGIN ISLANDS (US)	52.6
5	LESOTHO	38.0
6	JAMAICA	36.1
7	BELIZE	34.4
8	ST. KITTS & NEVIS	33.6
9	SOUTH AFRICA	33.0
10	GUATEMALA	31.2

TOP 10
Countries by Murder Rate per 100K Inhabitants 2014

12	COLOMBIA	27.9
19	PUERTO RICO	18.5
21	DOMINICAN REPUBLIC	17.4
23	PANAMA	17.2
26	MEXICO	15.7
108	UNITED STATES	3.9

Selected Hispanic Countries by Murder Rate 2014

Source: United Nations Office on Drugs and Crime

To put this into perspective, San Salvador, the capital of El Salvador, with a murder rate of about 116 per 100,000, is about twice as dangerous as the two most murderous U.S. cities per capita: St. Louis and Baltimore (with 59 and 51 murders per 100,000, respectively).[10]

Chicago, my hometown, has been historically violent as of late, reaching 762 murders in 2016. However, with 3 million people living in Chi-town, the city's murder rate is still "only" 25 per 100,000 people. As a country, it would place #15, just ahead of Brazil.[11]

10 *DIEZ*

Why do Hispanics have so many last names?

As a boy, I recall watching the famed golf tournament, the Masters, with my father. It was there I first heard the name of Spaniard José María Olazábal. I had never heard a name like that before.

> *Hey Dad—why does he have three names?*
> *And why does he have a girl's name?*
> *Or is "María" his last name?*
> *And if so, where did "Olazábal" come from?*

My father told me to be quiet and watch the birdie putt.

Several years later, as I studied the language and culture, these answers were revealed to me. Apart from general knowledge about something extremely personal to people—their last name(s)—understanding Hispanic naming conventions is critically important for business purposes.

Namely, proper documentation on employment forms. When bad things happen (injuries, deaths, Immigration and Customs Enforcement raids, to name a few), minor errors in your record keeping can cost millions.

New-hire paperwork can be lengthy, tedious, and confusing for anyone, especially so for those with different language preferences and limited reading and writing skills.

From I-9 forms to insurance documents to tax filings, your new-hire practices will likely account for some language barriers. For Spanish-dominant workers, I recommend my clients use Spanish application forms with English subtitles. In this way, if the applicant needs assistance, an English speaker can still help while examining the same document.

But let's not get ahead of ourselves—it all starts with getting the name correct. Let's return to our two-time Masters champion as an example, whose full name is actually José María Olazábal Manterola.

José María Olazábal Manterola

José is easy enough—it is the Spanish equivalent of Joseph and forms the first part of his first name.

María is the Spanish form of Mary. In this case, María is the second part of a compound first name, tag-teaming with José in tribute to the parents of Jesus Christ: Joseph and Mary—José María. Although this naming convention is not readily used in English (I have never met a "Joe Mary Johnson," personally), José María is somewhat common in Spanish.

So, José María is his first name.

Olazábal is his father's family name, also known as his primary last name. Similar to English culture, we typically take our father's family name as our last name. Same rule applies in Spanish.

Manterola, then, is his mother's last name. For accurate record keeping, both last names are important, so make sure both are included on official records.

So, to recap:

José María Olazábal Manterola

First name   Primary last name   Mother's family name
               (Father's family name)

New *vocabulario* for administrators.

English speakers are accustomed to looking at the *last* last name (that is, the name positioned at the very end) and assuming it is the primary last name.

In our example, it would be logical for an English speaker to look at *José María Olazábal Manterola* and think, "There's not much room on this form. Let's keep it simple, *José Manterola*."

Sharing your assumption with him could be perceived as clueless or disrespectful—or both. What's more, from a business standpoint, this error could have far-reaching consequences if bad things happen. An excellent HR administrator once told me, "My job is to assume that not only are good things *not* going to happen, but terrible things are *sure* to happen." And if something bad *does* happen—for example, someone gets injured on the job— and your records aren't accurate, that could lead to fines or other major headaches.

It is a depressing way to view the world, but a necessity for your colleagues who are responsible for hiring. These individuals on your team should remember the word *penultimate*—second to last.

When examining the name *José María Olazábal Manterola*, the penultimate name—Olazábal—is the primary last name. For more practical purposes, hyphenate the two last names (for example, Olazábal-Manterola) when creating personnel files, thus avoiding the unconscious temptation of looking at the wrong name.[12]

PENULTIMATE
(next to last)

José María	Olazábal	Manterola
First name	Primary last name (Father's family name)	Mother's family name

Do this but not that!

Given the confusion around these naming conventions, Hispanics often deliberately provide their mother's family name, thinking that is what English-dominant companies prefer for their records.

For this reason, your team should ask Hispanic candidates for their name as it appears on their Social Security Card. However, do not ask *to see* the actual Social Security Card. This can be perceived as discrimination, which you want to avoid.

Cultures—*Plural.*

In this book, we will examine common attributes that Hispanic cultures share, but it must be Noted—"Hispanic cultures" is plural. Each culture has its own unique aspects based on its history, geography, and leadership over the past several hundred years.

As a leader, it is your job to establish a baseline of understanding about the critical components of your business. The Hispanic workforce is one of those components.

Before you can embrace the Hispanic culture and drive competitive advantage, you must move your team from merely *recognizing* the importance of the Hispanic workforce to actually *accepting* it. The ten facts in this chapter are a great place to start.

To share these facts (and more) with your team, visit
www.goodtoexcelente.com and access free audio and video
content.

Now that we have reviewed the ten fundamental facts
about where we collectively stand, it's time to narrow our
focus to the top five countries of origin for Hispanics
living in the United States to get a better understanding
of each.

2

Understand the Origins

GOOD TO *EXCELENTE* FRAMEWORK™

AWARENESS OF CULTURE

RECOGNIZE + ACCEPT LA REALIDAD	UNDERSTAND THE ORIGINS	DISTINGUISH AMONG THE DIMENSIONS

AWARENESS OF LANGUAGE

SECRET OF THE SPANISH TWINS	EMBRACE THE EQUATION	FORWARD WITH (MICRO) FLUENCY

We have such a tendency to rush in, to fix things up with good advice. But we often fail to take the time to diagnose, to really, deeply understand the problem first. If I were to summarize in one sentence the single most important principle I have learned in the field of interpersonal relations, it would be this: Seek first to understand, then to be understood.

—Stephen R. Covey,
The 7 Habits of Highly Effective People

UNDERSTAND THE ORIGINS

FOR A MOMENT, THINK OF YOURSELF as a marriage
counselor.

A couple walks into your office looking for your assistance
in improving their compatibility. Both sides characterize
the relationship as, for the most part, *decent*. They work
together daily, coexisting in general harmony. However,
you can sense much is left unsaid. You feel a general
wariness and tension, while acknowledging that both
sides understand they need each other.

They plop down on your brown leather couch and look at
you expectantly. "Help us," they say in unison.

Where do you start?

Logically, you'll want to know the backstory—how they
met, how they started working together, the power
balance in the relationship, and the meaningful events
that led to where they are today.

And because you charge by the hour, you encourage the
couple to start talking—fast.

This is what we will do here. In this chapter, Understand
the Origins, we will visit each of the top five countries of
origin for Hispanics living in the United States to better
understand each one within its own historical context.
After establishing a current state of the union, we will
provide a glimpse of each country through five different
lenses:

Person Place Event Concept Dish

Now, I know what you might be thinking . . .

How could I even consider attempting to reduce the historical context of *any* place to a mere few hundred words? Would it be fair, you might argue, to forcibly distill the rich history of the United States of America to a few paragraphs on Plymouth Rock, George Washington, slavery, 9/11, and the hot dog?

COUNTRY / TERRITORY	% OF TOTAL
MEXICO	64%
PUERTO RICO	9.6%
EL SALVADOR	3.8%
CUBA	3.7%
DOMINICAN REPUBLIC	3.2%

Source: U.S. Census Bureau

No, of course not.

The goal here, though, is not to present a collectively exhaustive history. If you want that, go grab an encyclopedia.

No, the goal in this chapter is to provide immediate insight and context for certain places that are often lumped together in our minds. Learning about the Mexican–American War as a sophomore in high school may have been a state-mandated requirement, but it was perhaps of little value then.

Here you will receive the *Reader's Digest* version to help you quickly start learning more about the Hispanics on your jobsite, the cultural influences that drive their behavior, and why taking a little time to learn about them helps build trust—and, ultimately, a better working relationship for everyone.

For example, I often ask Red Angle workshop participants what they know about Puerto Rico. Typically I hear something like this:

It's an island.
I can travel there without a passport.

It is not a state, but the U.S. controls it.
It may be bankrupt. . .

Does that sound about right?

While it might not be the most comprehensive educational
exercise, the goal here isn't to prep you for a college
history exam. The goal is to expand your practical and
functional knowledge about a place like Puerto Rico in
just a few pages.

Remember, since I have committed to providing you the
MED (the minimum effective dose), each section is brief—
just a handful of carefully curated paragraphs for each
country of origin.

You're busy, I get it. Let me help enlighten you quickly so
you can get back to doing what you need to do.

¿Comprende?

Bueno. Now let's begin.

1 Mexico

"So far from God, so close to the United States."[1]

Status Update

Mexico, with a population of about 123 million, is roughly three times the size of Texas. It's also the 10th most populous country in the world, right behind Japan and Russia. Mexico has a trillion-dollar gross domestic product (GDP), making it the 15th largest economy in world.[2]

However, its GDP per capita—a broad, if imperfect, measure of standard of living—at around $9,000, ranks 63rd. Poverty continues to be a major national challenge. More than half of all Mexicans live below the poverty line (52.3 percent[3]).

The United States travel advisory website begins its out-line of Mexico this way: *Millions of U.S. citizens safely visit Mexico each year for study, tourism, and business, including more than 150,000 who cross the border every day.*

That being said, the United States deems only 9 of the 32 federal municipalities in Mexico to be safe for tourists. The remaining 23 municipalities have clearly stated advisories in effect as a result of the various organized criminal groups that engage in narcotics trafficking and other unlawful activities throughout Mexico.

The Global Competitiveness Report 2016–2017, published by the World Economic Forum, describes Mexico this way:

Mexico improves six positions to 51st place, mainly driven by gains in market efficiency. Primary education continues to be a significant competitive weakness compared to regional and global leaders, and institutional quality is lagging. The Mexican economy has been hit by falling oil prices, weak global trade, and a resulting fall in industrial production. However, it is still one of the most competitive economies in the region and is making progress on some of the fundamental drivers of future prosperity.[4]

Person :: Benito Juárez (1806–1872)

Known as the Abraham Lincoln of Mexico, Benito Juárez was born poor in the southern state of Oaxaca (wah-**HA**-kah). After earning his law degree, he entered into politics and eventually became governor of his home state, in 1847.

A decade later, he was appointed president of Mexico's Supreme Court, which, at that time, made him next in line for the presidency. A year later, in 1858, he became the 26th president of Mexico.

Once in office, Juárez went about separating church and state by curbing its revenue sources and limiting the Church's real-estate holdings. This move primed Mexico for growth as a nation but, naturally, made him an unpopular fellow at Sunday mass.

Juárez was unpopular in France as well. When his government "suspended payments of its foreign debt"[5]—a euphemism for *not gonna pay*—the French teamed up with Juárez's political rivals to seize control of Mexico. War raged for six years before the French finally relented.

It was during this time—the Franco–Mexican War—that the Battle of Puebla took place, on May 5, 1862. Outnumbered and outgunned, Juárez's forces secured an unlikely victory. Annually, this battle is celebrated in the Mexican state of Puebla but is not celebrated widely outside the state.

In the United States, however, May 5 arouses a bit more fanfare, where Americans across the country can be found celebrating by drinking heavily, wearing sombreros, and perpetuating the myth of this date as the "Mexican 4th of July." You may recognize it by its more common, Spanish name: **Cinco de Mayo**.

Note: Mexico's *actual* Independence Day is September 16.

Benito Juárez is remembered for valiantly fighting off the French occupation, but his legacy is not without controversy. Juárez had trouble accepting that he would one day no longer be president. So he kept running for office, eventually serving five terms as president and centralizing unprecedented power in the role. Today, Mexican presidents serve a single, six-year term in office.

Place :: The Mexican state of Coahuila

We hold these truths to be self-evident: (1) there are (at least) two sides to every story, and (2) history is written by the victors.

When evaluating relations—past and present—between the United States of America and *los Estados Unidos Mexicanos*, it all starts in the Mexican state of Coahuila (koh-ah-**WEE**-lah).

Nestled under the western half of Texas, Coahuila (along with Sonora, Chihuahua, and Tamaulipas) is one of the Mexican states that comprise the majority of the U.S.–Mexico border.

Before we go any further, let's just set the scene for what's been brewing north of the border . . .

In 1765, the American Revolution kicked off our country's efforts to separate itself from its English forbearers. On July 4, 1776, we sealed the deal and initiated our independence as a nation (though, we still fought the good fight for another eight years). Eventually, we adopted the Bill of Rights, in 1791, spelling out our most basic freedoms.

Soon after, Americans moved west from the original 13 colonies, beating back Native American Indians as they went. With the Louisiana Purchase, in 1803, from the French, we doubled the size of our nation. And soon after that, we picked off Florida and parts of Mississippi, Alabama, and Louisiana from Spain. Gradually, the American economy shifted into high gear, driven by industry in the North and cotton in the South, the latter being an extremely profitable business sustained by the no-wage labor of slaves.

By the 1830s, the young American nation was in full-growth mode. There was even a name for it: *Manifest Destiny*. Manifest Destiny was the notion that our nation was destined to extend "from sea to shining sea." Which was convenient, because America—for reasons partly due to the growing rift between the North and the South over slavery—desperately needed more real estate.

Texas, having earned its independence from Mexico in 1836, was an option, but all other lands in the Southwest were owned by Mexico. In 1846, U.S. president James K. Polk initiated a negotiation to purchase the states of the southwest from Mexico. Mexico's answer was more or less "thanks, but no thanks."

So, POTUS Polk picked a fight.

Polk ordered U.S. troops to advance into a disputed zone between the Rio Grande and Nueces Rivers, an area that both countries had previously recognized as part of the Mexican state of Coahuila.[6]

The Mexican Army did not take kindly to this offensive measure. They attacked, killing a dozen American soldiers serving under the command of U.S. general Zachary Taylor (who would succeed Polk as president three years later).

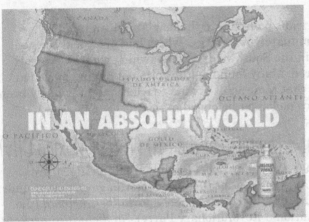

This Absolut Vodka ad from 2008, depicting the U.S.–Mexico borders prior to the Treaty of Guadalupe Hidalgo, led to many spirited historical discussions about the events leading up to the Mexican–American War.

The U.S. Army brought in reinforcements and entered Mexico, marking the first American war to be fought on foreign soil. Less than two years later, the Treaty of Guadalupe Hidalgo was signed, ending the Mexican–American War. Mexico reluctantly recognized the annexation of Texas by the United States and lost roughly one-third of its land, including parts of present-day New Mexico and Colorado, as well as Nevada and California.

History is often in the eye of the beholder, or so they say. Americans claim the Mexicans fired the first shot, lost the subsequent war, and signed the treaty. That's how nations are formed. Fair and square.

Mexicans, however, believe they were provoked into a war perpetrated by the United States to fulfill its Manifest Destiny. When it was over, the Americans *took* what they initially requested to buy during the pre-war negotiation.

Shortly thereafter, in 1849, gold was found in California (hence the "49ers," who rushed out West to nab the nuggets) and Manifest Destiny was achieved.

Americans poured into the new American territory. Unfortunately for Mexico, which had previously owned land in the Southwest, its landowning rights were not honored. Many found out (despite not having moved an inch) that their acres of land in what had previously been Mexico no longer belonged to them.

Event :: The birth of the PRI (1929, Mexico City)

In 1990, Peruvian Nobel Prize laureate in literature Mario Vargas Llosa called the Mexican government under the PRI, or *el Partido Revolucionario Institucional* (the Institutional Revolutionary Party), *"la dictadura perfecta"* ("the perfect dictatorship").[7]

To place the PRI in context, imagine for a moment that Republicans[2] had maintained uninterrupted control of the U.S. presidency, the Senate, and the House of Representatives for more than seven decades, only just recently being dethroned in the year 2000.
That is what happened in Mexico.

Since the founding of the PRI, in 1929, the party maintained a monopoly on Mexican politics, functioning as the state political party. Its colors—green, white, and red—matched the Mexican flag. From state governors to nearly every seat in the senate, the PRI roster utterly dominated the political scene. For decades, PRI leadership and the sitting president handpicked the next president of Mexico.

Dynasties like this don't persist without fraud and corruption. From 1929 to 1982, the PRI won every presidential election by well over 70 percent of the vote—margins that were usually obtained by massive electoral fraud.[8]

Lázaro Cárdenas, president of Mexico from 1934 to 1940, was one of Mexico's most popular presidents. He nationalized oil interests and created PEMEX (*Petróleos Mexicanos*, or "Mexican Petroleums"), employing hundreds of thousands of Mexican citizens over the years. Consistent with nearly every state-run oil business in the history of the world, massive corruption followed as the business returned billions in annual revenue.[9]

The current Mexican president, Enrique Peña Nieto, is a member of the PRI and his presidency has been marked by corruption charges, most notably a $7 million home-purchase scandal. [10]

Concept :: The plaza system

Over the past few years, many Americans have learned a great deal about Mexico through the trials and tribulations of Joaquín Guzmán Loera, better known as *El Chapo* (or "Shorty").

Actually, that is somewhat of a misleading statement. In the case of El Chapo, there were rarely actual trials (assigned judges were more often murdered), and "tribulations" implies some level of actual suffering. It is highly improbable that El Chapo suffered very much in prison.

Getting out wasn't too much of a chore either. To draw a quick contrast, consider the protagonist prisoner Andy Dufresne in the 1994 film *The Shawshank Redemption*, who used a rock hammer and a Rita Hayworth poster to dig his way through his prison cell wall and then army crawled through a quarter mile of shit before earning his freedom.

How did El Chapo escape last time?

He simply lifted up the base of his shower, descended a small ladder to an underground tunnel, and ambled less than a mile to freedom.[11] Also relevant to this incredible tale is this fact: next to the Mexican prison that had held El Chapo was a Mexican Army Base. What are the odds?!

(Note: El Chapo was captured for the second time on January 8, 2016. In early 2017, he was extradited to the U.S. to face six indictments related to drugs, money laundering, and firearms.[12] Time will tell, but an escape from a U.S. maximum security prison will probably be more challenging for Shorty.)

As my grandfather would shout, "Ahhh, they're all in cahoots!"

That may be true, but *how* are they in cahoots? What kind of system is in place to enable this level of cooperation?

The answer—linking everyone from the local police to drug kingpins to even presidents—is something called the plaza system. In his book *El Narco: Behind Mexico's Criminal Insurgency*,[13] author Ioan Grillo writes:

> *The plaza system is crucial to understanding the modern Mexican Drug War . . . In each plaza, a figure emerged who would coordinate the traffic and negotiate police protection. This plaza head could both move his own drugs and tax anyone else who*

smuggled through his corridor. In turn, he would
handle the kickbacks to police and soldiers, paying
for his concession.

The kickbacks make their way back up the chain of command to the highest levels of government, the *Partido Revolucionario Institucional* (PRI). Remember them?

Being in power for 71 straight years allowed the PRI to sufficiently work out the kinks. The plaza system is so successful because the extortion and narcotics taxes are accepted at the local level—the towns and cities, small and large, that interconnect Mexico—and because the most important of political elements is built into the system: plausible deniability.

As the money is distributed throughout the PRI hierarchy, officials don't know where the money is coming from. But they don't need to know, nor do they care to know. The further from the source, *los narcos* ("the drugs"), the better. As long as the money flows, everyone is happy.

Political infighting and territory gerrymandering is secondary when the demand for your products is so great. Like any profitable business, the focus is on satisfying customers. And there is no shortage of customers for Mexican narcotics. The United States has a near insatiable appetite for illegal drugs coming from Mexico.

Recognizing the fundamentals of supply and demand, the plaza system encourages everyone to get along. Grillo explains:

> *Accounts show that police were the top dogs in the deal. Officers could smack gangsters around and, if they got too big for their boots—or showed up on the DEA radar—take them down. Police could also bust anyone who wasn't paying their dues, showing that they were fighting the war on drugs and clocking*

seizures and arrests. The system ensured that crime was controlled and everyone got paid . . . Everyone respected the hierarchy, and if any official couldn't keep order, he could simply be replaced by another aspiring PRI member.

Dish :: Tacos al pastor

You're likely already familiar with burritos, enchiladas, tamales, and traditional tacos, so next time impress your Mexican friends by ordering *tacos al pastor* (ahl pah-**STOHR**), or "shepherd style."

Image ©IStockphoto – Rez Art

Think of tacos al pastor as the Mexican gyro, with a few important differences. As with a traditional Greek gyro, the meat in tacos al pastor is sliced from a spit—the rotating, vertical grilling method seen in gyro joints. But despite the reference to shepherds, this dish from Central Mexico is made from pork, not lamb. The pork is marinated in a mixture of dried chilies, spices, and pineapple, providing a memorable zing. When ready to serve, the pork is sliced into thin strips on an open tortilla, which is then garnished with chopped onions, salsa, and often pineapple.

2 Puerto Rico

Cuba

Dominican Republic

Puerto Rico

Haiti

Honduras

The rich port.

Status Update

Overshadowing all the beauty in Puerto Rico is the ugly reality of the Puerto Rican economy. After defaulting on billions in debt in 2015, the island economy fell into a downward spiral. How and why that happened is just another element of the complicated relationship between Puerto Rico and the United States.

After assisting Puerto Rico with its liberation from the Spanish crown in 1898, the United States simply never left. And unlike with Cuba (which we'll visit next), the United States chose to maintain control over its affairs.

The U.S. Congress wielded its control over the island and in 1976 granted tax incentives that made Puerto Rico an attractive locale for manufacturers and Big Pharma. Twenty years later, Congress began phasing out those incentives, until they eventually expired—which brings us to 2006.[14]

Poor fiscal management (the Puerto Rican government learned the hard way that revenues should *exceed* expenses) and continuous bet-the-house debt structures resulted in the island's economic decline. And the Great Recession only accelerated the downward spiral Puerto Rico was already in.

In just 15 years' time, Puerto Rico's debt *tripled*.

Whereas American municipalities and their utilities can declare bankruptcy, the same isn't true in Puerto Rico. And although the American government helped create the mess for this "state but not a state," many American entities (corporations, hedge funds, pensions) own bonds on the Puerto Rican debt, so it's a *Catch-Veintidós* (ahem, "Catch-22").

As poverty rates approach 50 percent, thousands of Puerto Ricans, who are natural-born citizens, are moving to the United States in record numbers. This further exacerbates the revenue shortfall of the Puerto Rican government since there are fewer people to tax.

This is the current Puerto Rican death spiral playing out in real time.

The U.S. Central Intelligence Agency (CIA) reports that public debt rose to 105 percent of GDP in 2015, about $17,000 per person, or nearly three times the per capita debt of the state of Connecticut, the highest in the United States.[15] The reality is, this wouldn't happen if Puerto Rico was a full-fledged state in the union. But it's not. The story of how we ended up here is essentially the history of Puerto Rico.

Event :: Puerto Rican "Freedom"

By the mid-19th century, Cuba and Puerto Rico were the two remaining islands in the Caribbean still under Spanish rule. The United States was committed to limiting the reach of Spain in the Western Hemisphere, culminating with the Spanish–American War.

After assisting Cuba with its independence from Spain, in 1898, the United States turned its naval attention southeast to Puerto Rico. In only a few weeks, the roughly 1 million Puerto Rican citizens were, after 400 years, finally free of Spanish rule.

In the Treaty of Paris that followed, Spain relinquished sovereignty over Cuba, setting the table for Cuban self-rule. Puerto Rico, however, along with the Philippines and Guam, were *ceded* to the United States.

The semantics here are important. Spain *relinquished sovereignty* over Cuba. To relinquish sovereignty means to allow for a self-governing state.

Puerto Rico, however, was *ceded* to the United States. That is, Spain *gave up* Puerto Rico. Which begs the questions, to whom did Spain give up Puerto Rico?

To the Puerto Ricans themselves?
Not quite.

American forces helped rid Puerto Ricans from Spanish rule ... and then installed themselves as rulers.

Why did they do that?

For one, Puerto Rico was strategically located. It would serve as an ideal way station for ships heading into the Atlantic. Puerto Rico's sugarcane was also critical to the American diet. Formally controlling those elements—in addition to the tariffs and exchange rate—would significantly benefit the United States.

American leaders did not think Puerto Ricans had the ability to self-govern.

In *Latino Americans: The 500-Year Legacy That Shaped a Nation*, author and PBS NewsHour senior correspondent Ray Suarez writes:

> *After dismissing the island's educated elite as unsuited for and uninterested in U.S. democracy, he [one S.S. Harvey, writing a letter from Ponce to be published in the New York Times] "praised" the common people as "light-hearted, simple-minded, harmless, indolent, docile people, and while they gamble and are fond of wine, women, music, and dancing, they are honest and. . . Let us educate these people, and teach them what government of the people means. They do not know, and never will, unless the people of the United States teach them."* [16]

That attitude, nearly 120 years later, has had far-reaching consequences that still demand thoughtful analysis and commitment.

Person :: Isabel González

As Americans assumed control over Puerto Rico, there was an obvious gray area regarding the island's citizens. Puerto Ricans were not U.S. citizens. They were *like* U.S. citizens, but not officially.

In 1902, a 20-year-old Puerto Rican by the name of Isabel González forced the issue. While she was on a boat from San Juan, Puerto Rico, to New York to join her fiancé, the immigration commissioner for the U.S. Treasury issued a new regulation changing the status of travelers such as González to that of foreigners, aliens. She was now to be treated like a new arrival from a foreign country, with discretion given to immigration authorities over whether the immigrant would be a desirable presence in the United States.[17]

Immigration law at the time had a simple, four-part checklist to determine the desirability of any one individual. The following types would be denied entry:

- *Idiots*
- *Insane persons*
- *Paupers*
- *Persons likely to become a public charge*

As far as immigration requirements go, I like the brevity, but it seems open to broad interpretation . . .

Isabel González was denied entry due to reason #4. González was 20, unmarried, pregnant, and had less than ten bucks in her pocket.

A trial ensued. Friends and family of González testified on her behalf. Unfortunately, her fiancé could not attend the trial, because he couldn't take off work, which proved damaging to her case.[18] Isabel González was denied entry to the United States a second time.

Undeterred, González and her legal team switched tactics. They would no longer argue about the definition of a public charge. Instead, they decided to take a stab at the *elefante* ("elephant") in the room.

If Spain ceded Puerto Rico to the United States, which then took control of Puerto Rico's commerce and appointed executives in Washington, D.C., to run the place, Puerto Ricans were now living in a part of the United States and were technically American citizens.[19]

The strategy worked. Isabel González won.

Sorta.

The court ruled that, as a Puerto Rican, González could not be denied entry to the United States. However, the court kicked the can down the road, as it were, and refused to rule that Isabel González was an American citizen.

Place :: New York City

In addition to the rights of citizenship resulting from the efforts of Isabel González, two other forces led to the Great Migration of Puerto Ricans to New York: World War II and air travel.

During World War II, manufacturers desperately needed laborers to replace the millions of workers called into the armed forces. Thousands of Puerto Ricans ably filled those openings in New York, and word of the opportunities in the United States returned to the island. In the coming years, millions more Puerto Ricans would emigrate to New York.

To better assimilate the arriving Puerto Ricans, the Migration Division of the Department of Labor of Puerto Rico opened its office in New York City in 1948. The department helped inform the newcomers about housing and the local job market.

In the decades to follow, *Boricuas*[20] (boh-**REE**-kwahs), or natives of Puerto Rico, represented nearly 80 percent of the city's Hispanic community and 12 percent of the city's total population.

Because of the aforementioned economic woes affecting the island, another wave of Puerto Ricans have been migrating to the U.S. While the

Puerto Rico Lost More Migrants to Mainland Since 2010 Than During 1980s or 1990s

Average island net migration per year

1980-1990 (10 Years)	1990-2000 (10 Years)	2000-2010 (10 Years)
-13,000	-11,000	-48,000

Source: Christianson, 2001 and U.S. Census Bureau 2013 population estimates.

PEW RESEARCH CENTER

Northeast United States remains a popular destination,
Puerto Ricans are also choosing to live in cities like
Orlando and Philadelphia in large numbers.

Concept :: The Jones–Shafroth Act

In 1917, nearly 20 years after the United States
dismissed Spain from its imperial duties on the island of
Puerto Rico, President Woodrow Wilson signed the *Jones–
Shafroth Act*.

The act read (and I'll paraphrase here):

> *Dear Porto Ricans,*[21]
>
> *We should have done this a long time ago—namely,
> immediately after we replaced the Spanish as the
> rulers of your fine little nation, er, commonwealth.
> From here on out—and retroactively for anyone born
> in Porto Rico since we Americans set up shop in April
> of 1898—Porto Ricans are U.S. citizens. Welcome to
> the United States (please Note: you are still definitely
> not a state).*
>
> *—President Woodrow Wilson*
>
> *P.S.: You may have heard about this little thing called
> World War I? Now that Porto Ricans are U.S. citizens, we're
> gonna need 20,000 of your best men to serve in the U.S.
> armed forces. We'll swing by in a month to begin boot camp.*

The cynic among us may view this timing as a little
suspicious. Twenty years after taking control of Puerto
Rico, we decide that March 2, 1917, is just the right time
to retroactively grant citizenship to its people. Exactly one
month later, on April 2, President Woodrow Wilson went
before Congress recommending a declaration of war
against Germany.

Dish :: Mofongo

In addition to being fun to say—go ahead, say it out loud, *mofongo* (moh-**FOHN**-goh)—this is one tasty dish. Mofongo represents the island of Puerto Rico's cultural fusion of native Taíno, African, and European strands that comprise the country's DNA.

Typically arriving on your plate in the shape of a 12-inch softball with a flattened base, mofongo is made of fried plantains and then smashed with salt and garlic (for the uninitiated gringos out there, plantains are *like* bananas just not as sweet).

Packed inside this plantain orb of deliciousness—or surrounding it on the plate—you will find any number of proteins: beef, bacon, *chicharrón* (think pork rinds), chicken, shrimp, or octopus.

Image ©IStockphoto – SM Pics

3 Cuba

Patria o muerte ("Fatherland or death").

Status Update

In December 2014, President Barack Obama began the restoration of diplomatic relations with Cuba. This historic announcement marked the easing of decades of hostile interactions between the two nations.

While many American would-be tourists welcomed this news by dreaming of cigars, rum, and '57 Chevy Uber-rides on the island, not everyone was happy.

Many U.S. lawmakers viewed the political shift as tacit endorsement of the communist Cuban dictatorship, which has been in power since 1959. As we'll discuss, the Castro regime has a brutal and oppressive history, responsible for killing thousands of its citizens.

Propped up for a few decades by the Soviet Union (before its collapse in 1991) and then Venezuela (before *its* collapse in 2014), Cuba under the Castro regime has become a third-world country.

Power outages in Cuba are frequent. Transportation has improved little in the past few decades. Venezuela has provided cheap petroleum to Cuba in exchange for tens of thousands of medical professionals,[22] but that agreement has faltered as the price of oil has collapsed—as has the country of Venezuela itself.

Cuba's infrastructure is decades behind anything close to

what might be considered "modern," and the streets of Havana, its capital, are strewn with garbage and sewage, even as its housing market skyrockets—the only bright spot in the dismal Cuban economy.

Attempting to stem some of the dismal tide, the Castro regime has modified its stance on regulations, now permitting the private ownership and sale of real estate, new vehicles, electric appliances, and cell phones.

Person :: Fulgencio Batista

The Castro *hermanos* ("brothers")—Fidel and little bro Raúl—are well known, but what do we know about the individual who preceded them? Who was in power before the Castros, and what did that person do that inspired Cuba to support Fidel so enthusiastically?

Fulgencio (foohl-**HAYN**-see-oh) Batista was born to a humble, mixed-race family in eastern Cuba in 1901. At age 20, Batista joined the military and rose through the ranks. By the time he was 27, Batista was promoted to sergeant stenographer, which introduced him to the officers who would help him lead a successful coup five years later.

Despite the backing of the United States as Cuba inched toward democracy, the government of Ramón Grau—a doctor and academic turned politico—failed to consolidate power in 1933.

Cover of Time Magazine
April 21st, 1952

As violent riots erupted across Cuba, Batista seized power. After installing a puppet president, Batista became the chief of the armed forces until 1940, when he was officially elected president of Cuba.

The United States, impressed with Batista's show of strength and desiring an ally in the region to help stamp out communism, officially recognized the new government within a week and remained one of Batista's most important and faithful supporters until the late 1950s.

Since Cuba's constitution prevented presidents from serving two consecutive terms, Batista was forced to eat crow, relinquishing power back to the very guy he sacked in the coup—Ramón Grau. Peacefully stepping aside, Batista was elected to the senate as he made his second move toward the presidency.

Finding free elections to be less than predictable—and facing popular opponents like the young Fidel Castro—Batista staged a second coup in 1952, after which he promptly dissolved the country's constitution, suspended the right to strike, and outlawed political formations.

In 1953, Batista quickly and brutally stamped out Castro's first communist rebellion. To stimulate the economy (and line his own pockets), Batista turned Havana into the "Latin Las Vegas." He allowed large-scale gambling, which attracted wealthy Americans, as well as mafia bosses, who trafficked drugs through the city.

Wide-scale corruption and graft followed, led by Batista personally. U.S. backing of Batista remained strong, though, since American businesses thrived on the island. Playing the game, Batista held a presidential election in 1954—with himself as the sole candidate on the ticket.

Batista's dictatorship intensified. Media censorship—in the form of imprisonment and torture of political challengers, as well as increased military police presence in the streets—set the stage for much-needed change. Following another election in 1958, widely believed to be rigged, Batista finally lost the support of the United States, and the revolution was underway. On New Year's

Day in 1959, Batista fled to the Dominican Republic and left the Cuban people in the capable, criminal, and soon-to-be communistic hands of Fidel Castro.

Event :: The Bay of Pigs Invasion

If you were searching for a specific event in history when the relationship between the United States and Cuba became irreparably severed, the Bay of Pigs Invasion would be it.

Shortly after denouncing the dictatorship of Fulgencio Batista, in 1959, Fidel Castro introduced his own authoritarian government. From the American perspective, Castro was yet another in a long line of potential dictators-in-waiting from Hispanic nations who would have to be dealt with.

Americans typically have three general rules for foreign nations:
1. *Don't mess with American businesses.*
2. *Don't mess with American tourists.*
3. *Don't mess with American oil.*

In the 1960s, a fourth hot button was in place: *Don't even think about communism.*

While largely sparing American tourists (#2 above), Fidel Castro lit the fuse on the other three. After Cuba decided to buy its petroleum from the Soviet Union, the U.S.-owned refineries in Cuba countered by refusing to process it. Fine, said Castro, absorbing Uncle Sam's counter-punch. He then landed a haymaker of his own, seizing control of the refineries.[23]

In one fell swoop, Castro messed with American businesses and American oil in the name of communism. *No bueno*, said America.

Recruiting Cuban exiles, the U.S. Central Intelligence Agency (CIA) trained these men in the hopes of invading Cuba, overthrowing Castro, and eradicating the communist threat that loomed 90 miles from American shores.

The primary concern behind the Bay of Pigs Invasion—initiated by President Dwight D. Eisenhower and eventually bungled by President John F. Kennedy—was national plausible deniability. Deliberately interceding to overthrow a national government, while not unprecedented in American history, was not something we wanted to get caught doing.

So, with the goal of destroying Castro's military aircraft, the CIA repainted old World War II bombers to look like Cuban air force planes and then crafted an elaborate ruse. Claiming that a Cuban defector was attacking Cuba's own air force base in response to the Castro dictatorship, the United States was able to avoid any perceived involvement.

However, when photos of the disguised planes revealed that they were clearly not assets of the Cuban air force, President Kennedy was forced to cancel phase two of the invasion: the scheduled American airstrikes in support of the Cuban revolutionaries, who were already battling Castro's troops on the island.

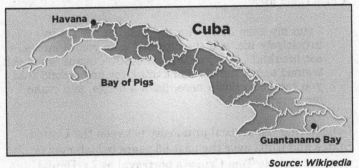

Source: Wikipedia

Hung out to dry in the swampy *Bahía de Cochinos*—or "Bay of Pigs"—the Cuban exiles never stood a chance. Some 20,000 Cuban soldiers were waiting for these neo-revolutionaries.

An estimated 75 percent of the Cuban exiles fighting in the Bay of Pigs Invasion ended up in Cuban prisons. Twenty months later, Kennedy negotiated their release, which included sending $53 million worth of medicine and baby food to the Cuban government. (I can picture how the deal went down . . . "Castro: All right, final offer: $53 million in cash, 12,000 gallons of Robitussin, and 642 pallets of Gerber baby food. Go heavy on the Apple & Apricots—Cuban babies love that.)[24]

Following the failure for the Bay of Pigs, Castro consolidated even more power in Cuba, capitalizing on the David-versus-Goliath narrative, which he rode out successfully until his final days.

Place :: Guantánamo Bay

Mention Guantánamo Bay, and two things come to my mind: 9/11 terrorists in orange jumpsuits, and Jack Nicholson in a tan officer's suit—albeit for very different reasons. I specifically recall one of my favorite lines of Jack's as Colonel Nathan R. Jessup from the 1992 film *A Few Good Men*:

> I run my base how I run my base. You want to investigate me, roll the dice and take your chances. I eat breakfast 300 yards from 4,000 Cubans who are trained to kill me. So don't think for one second that you can come down here, flash a badge, and make me nervous.

Considering the mutual animosity between the United States and Cuba over the past 65 years (which may or may not include Tom Cruise's portrayal as Lt. Daniel

Kaffee alongside Mr. Nicholson), how and why does the United States own part of the island that houses the infamous U.S. Naval base Guantánamo Bay?

In 1898, after assisting Cuba with the removal of the Spanish crown from the island, the United States decided it would like to have a naval base there . . . forever.

After squatting for five years, the United States secured a perpetual lease on the base, located at the southeastern tip of the island, from the Cuban government in 1903.

The yearly rent for *Gitmo* (as it is affectionately called) is a mere $4,085.[25] Keep this in mind when railing against the U.S. government's ineptitude at the international negotiating table.

Best of all, because the Castro government does not see the United States' lease on Guantánamo Bay as legitimate, it has refused to cash the annual checks since the Bay of Pigs Invasion, in 1961.

Guantánamo Bay has been a lightning rod of controversy as the United States has housed—and occasionally waterboarded— prisoners there from Afghanistan and Iraq. Gitmo has earned criticism, both internationally and domestically, for the mistreatment and indefinite detention of inmates.

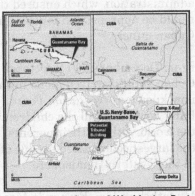

Image ©Washington Post

However, the smart money is on the United States keeping the base active. President Obama was unsuccessful at closing Guantánamo Bay during his two terms, and the Trump administration doesn't seem too keen on shuttering it anytime soon.

Concept :: Operación Pedro Pan

Shortly after Fidel Castro seized control of Cuba, in 1959, it became clear to many Cubans that the nation was headed from bad to worse. Fearful of more violence, political repression, and communist indoctrination, parents desperately searched for ways to keep their children safe.

In November of 1960, a Cuban man brought a 15-year-old boy to the director of the Catholic Welfare Bureau in Miami, Florida, Father Bryan Walsh. Recently arrived from Cuba, the boy, named Pedro, needed foster care. Aware of the deteriorating conditions in Cuba and the resulting rise in refugee migration to the United States (which included children), Father Walsh knew there would almost certainly be many more "Pedros" arriving soon. So he coordinated with then-President Eisenhower's administration, which ensured that government funds would be appropriated for the care of unaccompanied Cuban minors.[26]

From December 1960 to October 1962, more than 14,000 Cuban youths arrived alone in the United States. What is now known as *Operación Pedro Pan* (or "Operation Peter Pan," because of all the children who were cast out into the world without their parents), this mass migration was the largest coordinated exodus of unaccompanied minors in the Western Hemisphere.

My father-in-law, Fernando Meana, came to the United States as part of *Operación Pedro Pan*. He arrived in Miami at the age of 17 on one of the two daily Pan Am flights that shuttled Cuban youths to America. An only child, he would have to wait seven years before finally being reconnected with his mother. He never saw his father again. After spending a few weeks in Miami, my father-in-law was relocated to an orphanage in Marquette, Michigan, in the Upper Peninsula.

As sad as it was for my father-in-law and his father, their situation was an all-too-familiar reality for many in Cuba. Once the Castro regime had consolidated power and it became increasingly difficult to escape Cuba, many parents had to face the horror of never seeing their children again.

Concept :: The Triple Package

Despite the ongoing political chatter about the lack of upward mobility for minority groups in the United States, several manage to flourish consistently. How?

Amy Chua and Jed Rubenfeld, authors of *The Triple Package: How Three Unlikely Traits Explain the Rise and Fall of Cultural Groups in America*, examine the three characteristics they argue have lifted certain minority groups in this country.[27]
This is the triple package:

> 1. Superiority complex
> 2. Inferiority complex
> 3. Grit

In addition to Chinese, Nigerians, Mormons, Iranians, and Jews, the authors assert, Cubans have the triple-package DNA.

Superiority complex
Believing that you are better than other people is not a particularly popular sentiment to voice at a dinner party—but it *can* be an asset. When Castro took over Cuba, the professional, educated class (doctors, lawyers, academics, entrepreneurs) was the first to grasp where the future of Cuba was headed. These individuals were also the first to leave, which Castro encouraged.

The educated elite identified themselves as *political refugees*. They were driven from their home country by communist forces, enabled in no small part by the failure of the United States (see Event: The Bay of Pigs Invasion on page 81). Unlike other Hispanic ethnicities actively emigrating out of self-interest or opportunity, Cubans claimed they came to the U.S. because *they had to*.

More than semantics alone, the designation of "political refugee" provides preferential treatment under U.S. immigration statutes.

Furthermore, President Lyndon B. Johnson signed the *Cuban Adjustment Act* in 1966, which exempts Cubans from immigration quotas. Unlike other immigrants arriving in the United States, Cubans don't have to prove family ties. They only have to pass a criminal background check. After a year in the country, they may apply for legal permanent residence.

Inferiority complex
How can you have a superiority complex *and* an inferiority complex? It's more common than you might think.

The late co-founder and CEO of Apple, Steve Jobs, spoke openly about the effects of his adoption—about not being wanted. Andy Grove, former CEO of Intel, popularized the notion of perpetual paranoia despite massive success.

And have you seen Michael Jordan's acceptance speech into the National Basketball Association Hall of Fame?

Oh boy. It was your basic "look at me now" speech. As if someone like Michael Jordan needed to prove anything to anyone anymore.

Giant ego? Check.
Inferiority complex? Check.
Minority groups often share this same attitude.

This successful, educated class of Cubans landed in the United States with little or nothing. They had to start over. Doctors who were performing surgeries a month prior were now washing dishes for pennies a day. Professors who were mentoring PhD candidates seemingly yesterday were propping ladders in orange trees for 14 hours a day.

I can only imagine their urge to ask constantly, *"Do you know who I am and what I was in Cuba?"*

Grit

The authors of *The Triple Package* call it "impulse control," but what we're really talking about here is *grit. Stick-to-itiveness.* The drive to persevere despite the challenges. In a 2014 article, journalist Rick Sanchez notes:

> [Cubans] were able to work together to build wealth because of what they did share. Almost all Cubans arrived in the U.S. with a will to excel based on their resentment at what they had lost. They were all starting over. They've shared a history, a religion, a language, and a culture.[28]

My father-in-law is an example of grit. Before arriving to the orphanage in Marquette, Michigan, he had never seen snow.

And Marquette had never seen a Cuban.

With no winter coat and no English skills, my father-in-law worked hard. After graduating from high school, he moved to Chicago and attended college there. He developed his draftsman skills and later opened his own architecture firm. In the decades to follow, his firm became a million-dollar business, employing dozens.

Asked about it today, the 72-year-old responds with an unassuming shrug. It was what he had to do, he says. It wasn't easy, but nothing was going to stop him from achieving the American Dream, even if his dream initially was simply to go home.

My father-in-law's success is not an aberration. Within a few decades, Cuban exiles, starting from scratch, boasted more companies on the New York Stock Exchange than any other immigrant group.[29]

Among Hispanic immigrants, Cubans have higher levels of education and income. Rick Sanchez notes that the comparisons transcend Hispanic groups—by 2000, a mere four decades after arrival, there was a higher percentage of Cuban exiles earning more than $50,000 a year compared to white Americans.

Dish :: Paella

Paella (py-**AY**-yah), similar to many Cuban citizens, has its roots in Spain. Cuban-style paella, however, calls for a unique mix of ingredients including lobster and clams, as well as chorizo and chicken. The combination of seafood, meat, vegetables, and saffron-flavored rice creates an incredible dish, one my mother-in-law lovingly prepares twice each year for holidays.

Image ©IStockphoto - Lena Zap

4 El Salvador

The Savior.

Status Update

There is a certain not-so-subtle irony behind a country whose name means "The Savior" when the chances of meeting your maker increases significantly just by visiting it.

After a rise in violence in the summer of 2015, the current murder rate in El Salvador—the smallest nation in Central America[30]—is among the highest in the world, with an annual rate of 103.1 murders per 100,000 citizens for 2015.

As a comparison, the murder rate in the United States per 100,000 is 4.5.

Within the borders of El Salvador, the country's people face threats of gang violence in the form of kidnapping and murder. Outside the country, their relationship with Honduras—their much larger neighbor to the east—is just as tense. In fact, the entire region (El Salvador, Honduras, Belize, and Guatemala) is tense, as Honduras is the most murderous nation in the world per capita. El Salvador is second, followed by Belize (#5) and Guatemala (#8).[31]

El Salvador has been fraught with violence for decades. A civil war raged there for twelve years (from 1980 to 1992), killing more than 75,000 citizens and driving another 20 percent out of the country.

The Ronald Reagan administration was active in El Salvador's civil war, sending military advisers, financial aid, and arms to support the Salvadoran government against Marxist guerrillas.

Even though El Salvador, in 1992, formally (and publically) declared its country's civil war over, war rages on to this day, and much of the nation is in poverty. Political corruption feeds the social instability, most notably the arrest and imprisonment of ex-president Elias Antonio Saca on embezzlement and money-laundering charges in 2016.[32]

Yet despite these challenges, El Salvador's GDP has actually grown incrementally over the past two years. In September 2015, El Salvador kicked off a five-year, $277 million compact with the Millennium Challenge Corporation—a U.S.-government agency aimed at stimulating economic growth and reducing poverty—to improve El Salvador's competitiveness and productivity in international markets.

Person :: General Maximiliano Hernández Martínez

El Salvador has seen its fair share of totalitarian dictators, but General Maximiliano Hernández Martínez stands above the rest.

Hernández Martínez rose quickly in the military, earning the status of brigadier general by 1919. With a penchant for politics, he came into office as vice president in 1931, just as the Great Depression was devastating the Americas.

As coffee prices collapsed globally, demand for El Salvador's largest export suddenly vanished. The resulting lack of income exacerbated the divide between rich and poor. Nine months after becoming vice president, a military coup led to the arrest of Hernández Martínez.

As proof of his political talents, Hernández Martínez emerged from the coup as president, leveraging his military background for political gain among the rebels. Hernández Martínez was backed by the *cafetalera* ("coffee industry") oligarchy, which wanted to stop the growing communist presence in El Salvador and maintain its place at the top of the economic food chain.

While the coffee elites were pleased with Hernández Martínez, the peasants doing the work were not. Six weeks after the coup, a peasant rebellion erupted in the coffee plantations of western El Salvador. The 1932 insurgency was initially successful, taking control of several municipalities.

Then Hernández Martínez dropped the hammer.

In what is now known as *La Matanza* ("The Massacre"), the forces of Hernández Martínez murdered anywhere from 10,000 to 30,000 Salvadoran *campesinos* ("peasants"). Within a week, the rebellion was quashed and the dictatorship of Hernández Martínez was crystal clear to the nation of El Salvador.[33]

Despite his ruthless leadership, Hernández Martínez still managed to usher in stability and some advances to the nation. He created a national mortgage bank and established a central reserve. He also implemented women's suffrage.

However, the modest progress wasn't enough to counteract the brutal repression carried out by his regime—which, in the end, proved too much for even Hernández Martínez himself. He was ousted in 1944 after a revolt in May of that year. He fled to Honduras afterward and lived in exile until 1966, when he was stabbed to death by his chauffeur, whose father had been a victim of Hernández Martínez's dictatorship.

Even after his death, though, the brutal legacy of Hernández Martínez endured. The tactics he used while in power provided a violent playbook for future Salvadoran strongmen. And the message he had made so painfully clear to the peasant class—that any resistance to his regime would be stamped out by slaughter— contributed to the growing anger and resentment that eventually led to civil war decades later.

Event :: The 100-Hour War

Sports have a unique capacity to unite people. But much like the 1968 Philadelphia Eagles fans who threw snowballs at Santa Claus during a football game (yes, this really happened, by an aggrieved Eagles fan base who were none too pleased with their losing season that year), it can also bring out the worst in people.

In this case, the sport was *fútbol*, the year was 1969, and the setting was a trio of FIFA World Cup qualifier matches between neighboring nations El Salvador and Honduras, games that would plunge these Central American countries into all-out war.

Tensions were already high as more than 100,000 Salvadorans were living in Honduras illegally, desperately looking for employment opportunities. Thousands more had settled on the border between the two countries. Discussions of border enforcement and job-stealing undocumented workers abounded. Over the next 18 days, El Salvador and Honduras would battle on the pitch three times to determine who would qualify for the 1970 World Cup, to be played the next year just up the road in Mexico.

On June 8, in the Honduran capital of Tegucigalpa, the

Honduran national team won 1–0. Violence between the fans ensued.

One week later, in the Salvadoran capital of San Salvador, El Salvador issued a beatdown, winning 3–0. Once again, violence between fans ensued.

Nine days later in Mexico City, the rubber match was set. Winner take all.

This third and final match of the month of June 1969[34] required extra time. El Salvador won, 3–2. Violence between fans, predictably, ensued.

Less predictable, however, was the Salvadoran army, which commenced an air strike on Honduras, along with a ground invasion of the country. Four days later, the Organization of American States (OAS) broke up the fight, but not before the deaths of over 2,000 people on each side. In the end, more than 300,000 Salvadorans were displaced from their homes.

Although some viewed it as merely a regionally charged, sports-influenced aberration, the 100-Hour War reflected not only the social and political instability in El Salvador at the time but also the tensions that arise today all over the world as a result of a mass immigration of people competing for resources and a better future.[35]

Concept :: Mara Salvatrucha (MS-13)

As discussed earlier in this section, U.S. involvement in El Salvador's civil war was explicit. We were actively trying to enact change in a foreign country, which resulted in the unfortunate deaths of thousands. In other, more indirect methods, Uncle Sam has irrevocably contributed to the current state of affairs in El Salvador.

The Mara Salvatrucha, or MS-13, is one example.

Mara Salvatrucha is an international gang known for its brutality and a cultural moral code built on merciless revenge. The "Salva" in Salvatrucha is derived from El Salvador, while "trucha" means tricky, or street smart.[36] Instantly recognizable are the elaborate Mara tattoos that cover the bodies and faces of the gang's members.

In addition to Honduras, Mexico, and other Central American nations, *los maras* are the driving force behind most of the violence in El Salvador. Now then, can you guess the birthplace of MS-13? If your guess was somewhere in Central America—guess again.

It was actually in Los Angeles, California.

FBI.gov reports the presence of MS-13 in at least 42 states, and the District of Columbia and has about 6,000 to 10,000 members nationwide.[37]

Here's how it happened.

As the civil war in El Salvador raged for over a decade, more than 20 percent of the population fled. Many landed in California. With little structural support to integrate these political refugees, local gangs offered work, income, and a sense of family.

A devastatingly brutal family, but a family nonetheless.

As gang members tend to do, they racked up criminal records large and small. This placed many Maras on the radar of the U.S. Drug Enforcement Agency and the U.S. Immigration and Customs Enforcement. Between 2000 and 2004, tens of thousands of these Central American immigrants were deported to El Salvador.

Many of these American-raised Salvadorans arrived in El Salvador, a place they'd never known, with only their affiliations to *maras* (like MS-13 or its arch rival gang, M-18), to guide them. Under the Obama administration, more than 2 million deportees provided a natural recruitment and integration process for *maras* in El Salvador.

The Salvadoran government has been ineffective in reducing *mara* violence. In August of 2015, the BBC *Mundo* ("BBC World") reported that El Salvador's Supreme Court officially declared MS-13 and M-18 as terrorist groups. Living up to their new label, Salvadoran gangs took the lives of 220 people that week.

While there is relatively little media coverage in the United States on the topic, El Salvador and Honduras represent failed states—the governments are no longer in control of the gang violence driven by *los maras* that preoccupies the nations.

Place :: Joya de Cerén

El Salvador may be Jersey-sized, but it has its own beautiful shore with active and dormant volcanoes. One of the most impressive places to visit is Joya de Cerén (**HOY**-yah day say-**RAYN**), also known as the Pompeii of the New World.

Designated a World Heritage site by the United Nations Educational, Scientific and Cultural Organization (UNESCO), Joya de Cerén offers visitors a unique opportunity to glimpse how the Maya people of 1,500 years ago lived.

Joya de Cerén was founded in what is now La Libertad in El Salvador. In AD 600, an eruption from the nearby Loma Caldera volcano devastated the settlement yet preserved it under layers of volcanic ash. Discovered in 1976, this archeological site offers amazing insight into the daily life of a pre-Hispanic village and its inhabitants. Everything from a sauna to half-consumed ears of corn was preserved.

Joya de Cerén plays an important role in connecting modern-day Salvadorans with their indigenous past and serves as a famous reminder of their presence prior to the Conquista.[38]

Dish :: La pupusa

It is impossible to visit El Salvador—or have dinner at a Salvadoran household—without becoming acquainted with *pupusas* (pooh-**POOH**-sahs).

Pupusas are thick Salvadoran tortillas stuffed with a variety of ingredients, such as cheese, pork, refried beans—and anything else in a Salvadoran fridge.

If this sounds familiar, yes, a Salvadoran pupusa is similar to a Mexican *gordita* (sure, you can imagine the one at Taco Bell), but don't mention this to a Salvadoran.

Image ©iStockphoto – Calero

5 Dominican Republic

Cuba

Dominican Republic

Puerto Rico

Haiti

The birthplace of the Américas.

Status Update

The Dominican Republic is located in the Caribbean, in between two other countries on our top-five list: Cuba and Puerto Rico. The Dominican Republic occupies two-thirds of the island, while Haiti resides on the remaining western third.

With its beautiful landscapes and rich history, the Dominican Republic is the most visited country in the Caribbean.

The current president, Danilo Medina, took office in 2012 and has instituted a series of reforms that have had a positive impact on the economy. The country has been the fastest-growing economy in the Americas in recent years due to expanded mining operations and tourism.

Amidst the national improvements, though, heritage.org reports that corruption is a serious problem at all levels of government in the Dominican Republic, including the judiciary and security forces, as well as in the private sector.

Two similarities with the United States are immediately apparent in the Dominican Republic: income inequality and illegal immigrants. The poorest half of the population receives less than one-fifth of GDP, while the richest 10 percent enjoys nearly 40 percent of GDP.[39]

The Dominican Republic and Haiti share their Caribbean island, and race-based conflicts have been common. Due to Haiti's proximity, the competition for natural resources, and a historically fraught relationship between the two countries, the Dominican Republic has enforced stringent measures against Haitians perceived to be living in the country illegally.

In 2013, a ruling by the Dominican Republic Supreme Court that limited the rights of hundreds of thousands of unlawfully present Haitians (and their Dominican-born children) to obtain citizenship triggered international criticism.[40]

Person :: Rafael Leónidas Trujillo y Molina

When examining the history of the Dominican Republic, the conversation almost always starts and ends with Trujillo (trooh-**HEE**-yoh).

Trujillo is still considered one of the most corrupt and brutal dictators ever known in Latin America, rather impressive given his close proximity to the Castro brothers in neighboring Cuba.

Similar to many cases around the globe, Trujillo rose to power under the guidance and influence of the United States, only to be taken down decades later, in part, by those same forces.

The United States first occupied the Dominican Republic from 1916 until 1924 as a result of concerns about the instability on the island after the Dominican Republic gained independence from Haiti in 1844. As tends to happen with American nation-building efforts over time, public sentiment in the United States turned against our occupying another Caribbean island (see: Puerto Rico on page 70).

Trujillo joined the Dominican Republic National Guard in 1918 and established himself quickly, formally leading the country's national police force by 1928. By leveraging the national militia as a political tool, Trujillo successfully overtook the Dominican Republican government as president after a brutal campaign of torture and intimidation against political opponents. He then quickly dropped any pretense of a democratic political process.

Trujillo's ruthlessness became obvious in 1937 when he ordered a Haitian cleansing in the country, massacring thousands of Haitians living in the Dominican Republic. Using similar tactics employed by the Castro regime in Cuba, the Trujillo regime quickly tortured and exterminated any dissenters, while the media was strictly censored by Trujillo himself.[41]

His megalomania rising over his three decades in rule, Trujillo renamed the capital city of Santo Domingo "Ciudad Trujillo." The province of San Cristobal was updated to "Trujillo," and the nation's highest peak, Pico Duarte, was renamed, yep, you guessed it, "Pico Trujillo."

As news of Trujillo's dictatorship spread globally, it became harder for the United States to tacitly condone and enjoy beneficial trade relationships with him. At the same time, the oppressed nation began to push back against the *generalísimo*. By the early 1960s, Dominican dissidents were receiving arms and cash from the U.S. Central Intelligence Agency to speed the end of the Trujillo regime. And in 1961, Trujillo was assassinated.

Event :: The governorship of Christopher Columbus

You undoubtedly know the grade school rhyme about Columbus sailing the ocean blue in 1492. Columbus' second stop (after the Bahamas) was the island of Hispaniola, the future home of Haiti and the Dominican Republic. Like most newly "discovered" lands by Europeans, there was a native population that had already been living there for centuries.

Nonetheless, the capital city of Santo Domingo became the first colony, and Columbus served as its governor until 1499.

It is thanks to Columbus' arrival in Hispaniola that the Dominican Republic is thought of as the birthplace of the Americas. It boasts the first cathedral, hospital, and university in all of Latin America and the Caribbean.

Place :: Punta Cana

Punta Cana, located on the eastern-most edge of the Dominican Republic, is a city of about 43,000 that has become a popular vacation destination. With beaches facing both the Caribbean Sea and the Atlantic Ocean, Punta Cana has something to offer not only to its visitors but also to the natives who make a living there.

Concept :: Ecotourism

The Dominican Republic has been a leader in ecotourism, putting tourists to work to improve its natural habitats while raising awareness of the beautiful ecology around the island nation.

Ecotourism represents an effort both to stimulate the economy at a local level and to protect and restore the Dominican natural environment.

Tourists have the opportunity to become certified within a day and participate in a coral restoration project, which helps transplant fragments of coral to a nursery so that they may grow and be restored back to the reef.[42] This project provides jobs to local divers and raises awareness for the need to protect our coral reefs while also allowing visitors to contribute in a very meaningful way to their host country.

Dish :: Sancocho dominicano de siete carnes

Sancocho (sahn-**KOH**-choh) is a meat and vegetable stew. The fancier version calls for seven different meats (i.e., *siete carnes*), while a simpler sancocho can be made with beef alone.

In the Dominican Republic, *sancocho dominicano* represents more than just a tasty dish brimming with meat and veggies—it is symbolic of community and culture, seen often at baptisms and weddings.

Image ©IStockphoto – Juan Monino

FROM HISPANIC BACKGROUND TO CULTURAL FOREGROUND

Now that you have enhanced your understanding of the historical background that influences how Hispanics think—about themselves and the United States—we will now dive into the eight cultural dimensions that drive the behavior of Hispanic workers on the job.

3

Distinguish Among the Dimensions

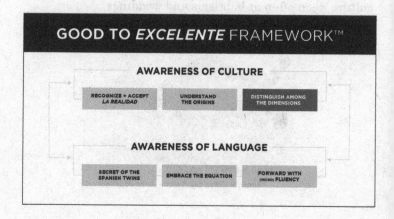

GOOD TO *EXCELENTE* FRAMEWORK™

AWARENESS OF CULTURE

| RECOGNIZE + ACCEPT LA REALIDAD | UNDERSTAND THE ORIGINS | DISTINGUISH AMONG THE DIMENSIONS |

AWARENESS OF LANGUAGE

| SECRET OF THE SPANISH TWINS | EMBRACE THE EQUATION | FORWARD WITH (MICRO) FLUENCY |

*We and They. Social scientists use the terms in-group
and out-group. In-group refers to what we intuitively
feel to be "we," while out-group refers to "they."
Humans really function in this simple way: we have
a persistent need to classify others in either group.
The definition of in-group is quite variable in some
societies, but it is always noticeable.*

—Geert Hofstede,
   Cultures and Organizations: Software of the Mind

Distinguish Among the Dimensions

THE CEO WAS PISSED OFF.

Despite his hectic schedule, he had carved out four hours of his morning to attend an award ceremony on-site. Yet when it came time for him to hand out the award on stage, the person being honored wasn't there to accept it, which left the CEO, in his words, "hanging in the friggin' breeze, looking like a Grade A jackass."

The project manager braced for fury as the CEO descended the makeshift dais. "I thought you said he was here!" the executive roared. "That was the whole reason I came! Why would I waste my morning handing out a trophy to a guy who isn't here?"

"Umm, sir. He was . . . he *was* here," the project manager stammered. "He just didn't want to come up to accept the award."

"Why the hell not?" The CEO asked as he unrolled the piece of paper in his hand. "Why didn't this, um, Roberto Rodriguez, want to shake my hand and accept this trophy if he was in the friggin' crowd? You nominated him based on his performance and work ethic, didn't you?"

"I know, sir. Yes. I agree," the project manager said, attempting to placate the executive. "It appears we missed some cultural elements."

"Which cultural elements," the CEO asked, enunciating with a deliberate lethargy, "did we miss? Tell. Me. Please."

Cultural clues
In this chapter, you will learn about some of the cultural forces that can affect behavior on the job. As you increase your understanding of these cultural elements at play around us every day—including those missed by the

managers in this story—you will start to recognize clues that will help you bridge the gap between what you *think* people should do and what they *actually* do. More importantly, you'll begin to understand why.

After all, it's incredibly hard to change human behavior when you don't understand what's driving that behavior to begin with.

While there is no shortage of books and articles on how culture influences behavior within organizations, this chapter has extracted the most relevant segments from the current research on cultural intelligence to improve your ability to persuade, influence, and establish trust with your Hispanic workforce.

This chapter will focus on eight cultural dimensions that cover a range of critical aspects of leadership. Here is a quick snapshot of what's to come:

1. **Individualism versus Collectivism:** *how individuals see themselves*

2. **The Power Distance Index:** *how individuals view and engage with those in positions of power*

3. **Competitive versus Collaborative:** *how individuals see the world*

4. **Uncertainty Avoidance:** *how individuals react to unstructured situations*

5. **Trust:** *how individuals develop trust for those outside their in-group*

6. **Persuasion:** *how individuals react to different styles of persuasion*

7. **Universalism versus Particularism:** *how individuals apply rules of conduct*

8. **Being versus Doing:** *how individuals differ when it comes to working to live or living to work*

Taken as a whole, these eight cultural constructs should help you better understand why people do the things they do—and how you can use that new knowledge to manage more effectively.

Dimension 1 :: Individualism versus Collectivism

The first cultural dimension we will review can be boiled down to a simple question: "Who am I?" Don't worry, we won't be meddling in metaphysics here—that's beyond the reach of this humble author. The answer to the question "Who am I?" is a binary choice, and its implications will reverberate throughout the other seven cultural dimensions—not to mention your jobsite.

And maybe even your incentive and award programs as well.

The *I* in "United"
The United States is a fairly individualistic place.
Well, check that. From a cultural standpoint, it might be one of the most individualistic places on Earth.

The founders of this great nation—searching for more religious freedom and fewer taxes—gave the middle finger to the King of England, floated across the Atlantic Ocean, cut down some trees, and began anew.

Then, in 1776, outgunned and outnumbered, we began to fight like hell for seven years to keep our independence. In 1783, Great Britain signed the Treaty of Paris, thus finally recognizing American sovereignty.

All in all, that is some fairly individualistic behavior. No question, individualism is in our country's DNA.

But how do we know just how individualistic Uncle Sam really is?

Can you determine statistically how far apart two cultures are? Can you quantify the difference between two cultures?

The answer to both of these questions is *yes*. And someone already has.

His name is Geert Hofstede. He's a Dutch researcher and a pioneer in cultural intelligence in the workplace. During a consulting stint with IBM in the late '60s and early '70s, Hofstede collected cultural data from around the globe, which he used to establish his theory on cultural dimensions within organizations.

Hofstede characterized the data along four dimensions, which we will review shortly. Of the 76 countries included in the IBM study, ol' Uncle Sam scored highest in terms of individualism.

We Americans are passionate about our individual freedoms— the freedom to say what we want, pray to whomever we want, and shoot whatever we want.[1]

Geert Hofstede, the godfather of cultural intelligence within an organization.

As we shift our thinking from national to cultural, I will refer back to Hofstede, the godfather of organizational cultural awareness.

"Freedom is an individualist ideal, quality a collectivist ideal," he notes.[2]

Fine then.
Consider it confirmed.

Uncle Sam is an individualist.
But aren't most cultures?

Citizens of the United States are a minority (culturally speaking)
In collectivist societies, people are integrated into strong, cohesive in-groups, in which members, throughout their lifetimes, continue to protect one another in exchange for loyalty, commitment, and cooperation.[3]

Individualism fuels American society. And although we might find this to be a familiar mind-set, we are still in the global minority. Over 70 percent of the people living on Earth live in collectivist societies.

Globally, collectivism drives the manner in which the vast majority of humans think and act.

While individualism drives American creativity and innovation—from Ford to Edison to Apple—it is important to recognize that other societies think differently.

Individualism versus collectivism is not a question of good or bad, right or wrong. They're just different.

"WHO AM I?"
A GLOBAL PERSPECTIVE

30%

70%

■ COLLECTIVIST
▨ INDIVIDUALIST

For collectivists, the focus isn't solely on *me*—it's on the group. Because harmony among the group is of the highest importance, your personal thoughts and feelings will typically take a back seat to those of the group's.

In a collectivist society, "groupthink" isn't negative, it's imperative.

As the diagram below shows, the United States is more than three times as individualistic as Mexico (with a score of 91 versus 30, respectively), which is closer in proximity to its Central American neighbors El Salvador and Guatemala. And while Guatemala, El Salvador, and Mexico are all culturally collectivist societies, there is a margin of difference among them in their own degree of cultural collectivism.

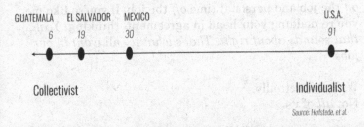

GUATEMALA	EL SALVADOR	MEXICO	U.S.A.
6	19	30	91

Collectivist   Individualist

Source: Hofstede, et al.

HOW DOES THE SCORING SYSTEM WORK?
Hofstede's scoring system is statistically based on a model called factor analysis. The details are confusing for non-quants such as myself, but the important thing to remember is that the country scores on the dimensions are relative. In other words, culture can be used meaningfully only by comparison.[4] There is no "good" or "bad" score—only observations and insights drawn from the relative distance between two cultures.

In Chapter 1, you read about the demographics underlying the reality that "They're not all Mexicans." Yes, 65 percent of all Hispanics in the United States are of Mexican descent, but another 20 million or so Hispanics are not. As you continue to explore the other seven cultural dimensions in this chapter, you will notice there are often wide gaps among Hispanic countries and their scoring on any one individual dimension.

Understanding these differences among Hispanics will enable you to think more deeply about your observations and help you identify the root cause of certain behaviors.

Survey says . . .

The IBM survey questions that Hofstede used to narrow in on individualism were focused on work goals. Individualists emphasized the importance of setting aside personal time outside of work, of maintaining the freedom to complete their work how they wanted to, and of having challenging work that enables a sense of accomplishment.

Challenging and rewarding work, partnered with freedom *on* the job and personal time *off* the job. If you're like me, you're nodding your head in agreement, thinking, *Yeah, that sounds about right. That's what we all want in our jobs.*

Well, no, actually.
Not *all* of us.

Collectivists, the survey revealed, emphasized the desire for on-the-job training to help improve skills, the need for adequate physical work conditions, and the importance of fully using the skills they've acquired.

In *Cultures and Organizations: Software of the Mind*, Hofstede et al. claim that individualists focus on elements that establish "independence from the organization." Personal time, freedom on the job, and challenging work all center around the individual employee.

Collectivists focus on the things "the organization does for the employee, stressing the employee's dependence on the organization."[5]

The Hispanic head nod

I often hear managers complain about what is sometimes called the "Hispanic head nod." The situation they're referring to is when instructions are given by a manager, and the feedback from the Hispanic workforce *seems* to convey an overwhelming sense of understanding.

All heads nod *yes.*

And yet when the manager returns later, he or she often finds that the work has been done incorrectly, incompletely, or not at all.

Why does this happen?

Part of the answer, as we'll see, has to do with this notion of collectivism, an overriding sense of trust within an in-group. Instead of trusting the manager's message on face value, the workers rely more on what is said *after* the manager finishes speaking, when the team determines the best course of action for themselves.

Hispanic workers might leave a manager's meeting saying something like:

> **¿QUÉ DIJO EL GUEY?**
> (kay **DEE**-hoh ayl **WAY**)
> What did the dude say?

Setting aside language barriers (which may be perceived or real), members of collectivist cultures will look for group consensus on next steps when instructions are provided from members outside of their in-group.

And make no mistake, English-speaking managers are definitely outside the in-group of Hispanic workers. We will talk more about the Hispanic head nod—and tips for how to address—in the second cultural dimension: the Power Distance Index.

Losing face
Growing up, my father often extolled to my brother and me a wise managerial maxim: *praise in public, criticize in private.*

Indeed, it is applicable across the globe. Simply put, no one (especially CEOs) likes to look bad in front of an audience. For collectivist cultures, this is doubly important. In collectivist cultures, the perception of the group is more important than that of the individual, so it is critical to avoid causing someone from a collectivist group to "lose face" or to lose respect in front of his or her peers.

I've seen it happen.

After a landscaping team misread the topography on a small commercial project and installed a portion of a retaining wall incorrectly, I witnessed a mid-managerial colleague verbally destroy the project foreman, who was Hispanic. Picture irate basketball coaching legend Bobby Knight on the basketball court at Indiana University, hurling a red plastic chair. But instead of a chair, imagine a three-foot juniper bush.

The rant, though brief, included references to this foreman's intellect and country of origin, as well as threats of deportation. The foreman's crew watched silently throughout the spectacle, eyes wide, taking it all in.

When I asked my colleague how that altercation might affect this leader's performance in the future, he said, "He's a big boy. He'll get over it."

Or not.

When a jobsite leader loses face in front of his team, it can irrevocably damage his ability to establish trust and manage his group.

Coaching: Three ways

I recommend a three-step strategy for improving your performance in coaching Hispanic workers who operate from a collectivist mind-set—regardless of their language of preference. As American managers, we tend to lead as individuals, while Hispanics more often follow as a collective group. Understanding this difference will help you coach situationally—alternating your style and technique depending on whom you are coaching.

First and foremost, remember to acknowledge the existence of your Hispanic workforce. This may seem obvious, but I assure you, it isn't always. Language barriers—perceived or real—can create distance between managers and employees, to the point where some Anglo managers might ignore Hispanics' presence on the job entirely. For example, when walking the job with clients, I'll often see Anglo managers acknowledge and say hello to white, English-speaking workers but fall silent and avoid eye contact when passing by Hispanic crews. This behavior, I've found, is driven largely by language barriers and by feeling insecure about addressing a group when you aren't comfortable speaking the group's language.

The good news is, as commonplace as this problem can be, it's not hard to remedy. It requires only a small amount of effort to nod or wave or smile—any subtle gesture that recognizes another's presence. And when done consistently, it can make a big impact on the morale of a team and the effectiveness of a manager. Humans aren't machines. If a manager's behavior when she walks by a Hispanic drywall crew is no different than it is when she walks by, say, a fleet of skid steers, the manager is missing an opportunity, albeit small, to build a connection.

It's a fundamental rule: you manage things and lead people. Develop the habit of acknowledging the presence of other human beings. Given the importance of group opinion among Hispanics, small gestures of acknowledgement and respect will travel quickly. Your efforts can influence the collective group, not just a single crew or individual. Nonverbal head nods, a small wave, or a basic introduction like the following work well:

¿CÓMO ESTAMOS, CABALLEROS?
(**KOH**-moh ay-**STAH**-mohs kah-bah-**YAY**-rohs)
How we doing, gentlemen?

Second, start rethinking the way you coach your
employees. Anglo managers are taught to coach
one-to-one—keeping it direct, simple, straightforward.
This coaching style makes sense in individualist cultures,
where the focus is on the one person. But it's often not as
effective in Hispanic, collectivist cultures, where the
group is more important. In collectivist cultures, one-to-
one coaching can cause someone to "lose face," like with
the project foreman of the landscaping team I mentioned
earlier. The important mind-set change for Anglo
managers to consider here is how to coach to a group
instead of a single individual.

When a coaching opportunity arises with an employee, try
to make it a group activity. Although only a single worker
might be in need of on-the-spot coaching, ask the entire
crew to pause for a moment to review something.
Addressing a larger group improves your chances of
clearer communication since the odds are greater that
someone in the group speaks both English and Spanish.
And in general, there's almost always someone else in the
crew who will benefit from the coaching as well.

Third, if the coaching doesn't improve performance, try
discussing the issue with the group leader, who may or
may not be the foreman. Within any group, there is
typically a tenured worker who has the respect of
everyone else. Explain the problem to this person and
enlist his or her help in correcting it. While this may seem
inefficient (like you are coaching from a distance), it can
be an effective technique within collectivist groups
because the pressure to conform—with improved
performance, in this case—is coming from within the
group.

Engagement versus feedback

As we've covered, Hispanic cultures generally value the group opinion. Harmony among the whole—in words and action—is of the utmost importance. This begins at birth, with the role of the family, and continues on through school.

In American schools, it's common for teachers to elicit participation from individual students by asking a question to the general class and waiting for someone to answer; children are encouraged to raise their hand and speak their mind.

Think about that for a moment. Does that sound like a common characteristic of collectivist cultures? Not so much, and with good reason. The value in collectivist cultures is on the opinion of the group—not any single individual.

Hofstede elaborates:

> *For the student who conceives of him- or herself as part of a group, it is illogical to speak up without being sanctioned by the group to do so. If the teacher wants students to speak up, the teacher should address a particular student personally.*

This thinking leads to predictable, long-term behavior. For anyone who has been training a group of Hispanic craft workers on the job, he or she finds out quickly that lobbing generalized pleas for engagement ("Just throw it out there, now. Whaddya think?") often results in awkward silence.

I recommend tapping into this collectivist mind-set. Organize the audience into small groups of 3 to 6 people and provide specific instructions on the feedback you expect. For example, when starting with a group of 20 people, your setup may sound like the following:

"Form five groups of four and write down three risks this job faces once we begin pouring concrete in July. Select one individual to read the answers your group came up with."

This technique may prove to be more effective because you are structuring the exercise around the group—not any single individual. The opinions of the group will surface, and one member (of their choosing) will voice the opinions of the group as a whole. This exercise fits nicely within the collectivist cultural paradigm.

Addressing the angry executive

Let's revisit our story at the beginning of this chapter involving the CEO, project manager, and the trophy-shy recipient, Roberto Rodriguez.

Are you getting a better sense now of why the Hispanic craft worker didn't rush the stage to accept his award from the executive? What was the company missing?

"People from the U.S. typically lead *as individuals* while people from Hispanic countries typically *organize as groups*. To lead Hispanics effectively, you will need to think in terms of groups. Being called out in front of your peers—for reasons positive or negative—is not desirable for members of collectivist cultures.

McDonald's and other global companies have discovered this cultural trait in highly-populated, collectivist countries such as China and India when "Employee of the Month" programs failed miserably. No one wanted to be employee of the month.

This isn't to say they didn't want to be exemplary employees. They simply didn't want to be singled out from the group—just like Roberto.

The CEO of Roberto's company, learning this cultural lesson the hard way, decided to make a change. Moving forward, the company would honor high-performing *crews*, not a single individual.

Hispanic cultures are collectivists, not individualists.
To lead Hispanic workers more effectively, think in terms
of *groups*.

Motivate in terms of groups.
Incentivize in terms of groups.
Reward in terms of groups.

Coach for improved performance . . . in terms of groups.

Do this and you'll avoid being left hanging in the friggin'
breeze, looking like a Grade A jackass.

Dimension 2 :: The Power Distance Index

IT WAS MY FIRST DAY ON THE JOB, during the first meeting of my professional career in the construction industry. The vice president of construction at the company was slowly dragging his eyes over the incoming class of managers he had recently hired. From all outward appearances, he did not seem thrilled with his decisions.

"I'll leave you newbies with two pieces of advice," he said sharply. "I hope to hell, for your sake, you follow them.

"First, you don't know shit about construction. But we've placed you with people who do, so ask questions and take notes."

I wrote that down.

"Listen to your trades, listen to your boss, and listen to your customer. Then, lastly, listen to yourself.

"And second, whenever you find yourself hating your trades, hating your boss, hating your customers, or hating yourself, remember this: *the quality you accept is the quality that sets the standard.*"

You could see the group of us collectively running this last phrase back and forth in our minds. "If you're smart," he continued, "that phrase will become more meaningful over time. It will point you in the right direction when shit gets jacked up on your jobsite."

As with all new hires, *shit did indeed get jacked up.*

That's how we learn.
That's how we become leaders.

But leadership, fundamentally, requires *follower*ship. If no is one following your lead, you are, by definition, not leading.

The Power Distance Index examines what less powerful members of a group expect and accept from their leaders in terms of inequality.

Let's break that phrase down into its two constituent parts.

Expect and *accept*. Keep these two words in mind. We know how critical it is to set expectations properly—with trades, bosses, customers (undoubtedly), and yourself. And without the acceptance from those you lead, there is no hope for actual leadership.

Inequality refers to the lopsided distribution of status, wealth, and power. The simplest question is this: Is inequality ever expected, accepted, or even desired?

To your average American, this question appears ridiculous.

After all, the United States of America was born out of its propensity to question authority—the English monarchy, as it were. The fundamental ideal of this great

Power Distance Index

COUNTRY	SCORE
GUATEMALA	95
PANAMA	95
MEXICO	81
COLOMBIA	67
EL SALVADOR	66
USA	44
COSTA RICA	35

Source: Hofstede, et al

nation is that *We, The People*, decide who manages our great nation. Not only do we have the desire to question authority, it is our responsibility to do so.

Questioning the divine right of bloodlines to rule the land, American revolutionaries did not expect, accept, or desire inequality. On the contrary, they determined that all men are created equal.[6] So why would anyone ever expect, accept, or desire *inequality*?

While it is rarely stated so bluntly, some Hispanic cultures actually do. Framed another way, Hispanic cultures have a high respect for authority and grant their leaders a wide degree of latitude.

Hispanics expect and accept a large distance between lower members of society and those at the top. This is the crux of the Power Distance Index.

Rich executives in the Ivory Tower. Peasants toiling in the fields. To Americans, this might sound like a recipe for revolt. But in high power distance cultures, all is right with the world here.

Take Mexico, for example. Remember the political party known as the PRI (*Partido Revolucionario Institucional*) from last chapter? Do you recall how many consecutive decades that party was in power?

Seven.

The PRI ruled for 71 consecutive years (1929–2000). After a brief hiatus, the party returned to dominance in 2012 with President Enrique Peña Nieto, who still commands the top post in Mexico.

Under the banner of the PRI, the plaza system was established, functioning to this day like a Swiss watch. In Mexico, corruption is not a cancer in the national corpus—it is the blood.

If corruption is obvious and known, why does it persist? In a word, *culture*.

In high power distance cultures, it is expected and accepted for the people in power to take advantage of their status. After all, leading people is challenging work; they deserve to skim a little off the top, right?[7]
The roots of Hispanic high power distance extend back to the birth of *caudillos* (cow-**DEE**-yohs). Caudillos were

charismatic militia men who earned the trust and respect of the public.

With their personal militia at hand, recruited from the local population, they defended the people. In return, they were exempt from taxes and criminal and civil prosecution.

80% *Percent of Latin American countries whose governments were military dictatorships between 1974 and 1989*

So, the charismatic strongman leads the local militia, pays little to no taxes, and cannot be tried in a court of law. When this scenario makes sense—when it is *expected* and *accepted*—this is what high power distance looks like. In your organization, though, it's a little different, right?

Or is it?

On the job
In my work leading Red Angle, I'm always fascinated with the range of different cultures represented by my clients. Within the confines of the American corporate world, there are high *and* low power distance cultures.

At one client, the CEO has no door to his office. He is accessible at any time. I've seen him giving high fives to interns during a hallway flyby. I've heard a project manager call him a "dumbass" following a poorly evaluated Fantasy Football trade—without fear of retribution.

This is a low power distance culture.

At this client, there is a relatively small power gap between lower members of the organization and those who wield the organization's power.

At another client, however, in the offices of the executive suite, you need a four-digit code just to open the frosted glass doors that lead to the executive assistants. In this culture, the CEO is revered, mentioned only in hushed tones. Calling this guy a *dumbass* would set off alarms and prompt a corporate-logoed SWAT team to repel from the roof and take you into immediate custody for questioning.

This is a high power distance culture.

Here, there is a relatively large gap between lower members of the organization and those who wield the organization's power.

What about results?
Do corporations from high power distance cultures perform better than those from low power distance cultures? Or vice versa? Not necessarily.

There is no evidence to suggest that one cultural mind-set delivers superior results over the other. The most effective corporations—and individuals—practice *situational leadership*. They adapt based on what their followers *expect* and *accept*.

The 23-year-old project engineer from Columbus and the 40-year-old craft worker from Colombia expect and accept different behavior from their leaders.

I still recall that leadership maxim I learned the first day on the job: *the quality you accept is the quality that sets the standard.*

The cultural dimension of the Power Distance Index tweaks this slightly: "The inequality the culture accepts is the inequality that sets the standard."

The question then becomes, what kind of workers are we leading and how does their culture affect their behavior?

Cultural dimensions 1 and 2: At a glance

At this point, we have now covered two of the eight cultural dimensions: Individualism versus Collectivism and the Power Distance Index. The graph below depicts the former on the *y*-axis and the latter on the *x*-axis and offers a striking visual at just how far apart the United States is in its worldview on two important aspects of culture that can affect behavior on the job.

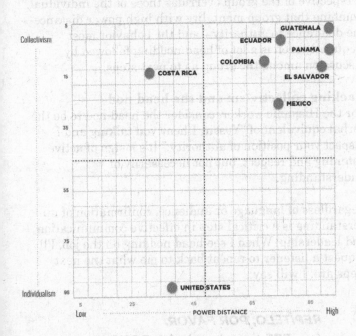

Collectivism . . . meet High Power Distance

In Red Angle workshops, I ask participants how often they hear the word "No" from Hispanic workers. For example,

- *No, I can't do the work.*
- *No, I've got a better suggestion.*
- *No, I don't understand your instructions.*

With some introspection, this is the most common response I hear:

"I hear *no* or get pushback from the Anglos every day, but I cannot think of a single time when I've heard that from Hispanic workers."

As you now know, collectivists identify themselves as members of a group first and foremost. The opinion and perspective of the group overrides those of the individual. Combine that group mentality with high power distance—the deference to authority—and the behavior most frequently seen is a lot of head nodding followed by discussion among the group as to next steps.

Hacking collectivism and the head nod

For the Hispanic worker, consider the head nod to be the verbal equivalent of "Yessir, I hear you talking and I respect your position of authority." It's a sign of active listening and respect, but not necessarily of understanding.

Regardless of language or audience, confirmation of understanding is a critical step in effective communication and leadership. When I see head nodding on the job, I'll request a listener to repeat back to me what the next steps are. I will say:

> ### REPÍTELO, POR FAVOR.
> (ray-**PEE**-tay-loh, pohr fah-**BOHR**)
> Repeat it, please.

You'll notice the *repite* (ray-**PEE**-tay) part sounds a lot like its English counterpart. This is what I call a Spanish Twin, which we'll discuss in more detail in Chapter 4.

The Spanish word *lo* means *it*; we're simply adding it to the end of *repite* to make a direct translation.

Fine, you might be thinking. *But you speak fluent Spanish. How do I know what they're saying when they respond?* Fair point.

In my experience, simply asking for Hispanic workers to "repeat it" in Spanish will provide some feedback for you to gauge their understanding. To ensure understanding in English, we will add two words:

en = in
inglés = English

REPÍTELO EN INGLÉS, POR FAVOR.
(ray-**PEE**-tay-loh ayn een-**GLAYS**, pohr fah-**BOHR**)
Repeat it in English, please.

Consistently asking these two small phrases will make a significant difference on multiple levels. First, Hispanics will come to expect that you will ask them to repeat directions back to them. Initially, this will be unusual behavior from a manager. In time, they will be prepared to engage instead of simply nodding.

Secondly, this interaction is very different from the routine where the manager saunters up, barks orders, and walks away. Engaging with workers in this way builds relationships and trust.

Lastly, both sides will learn new language skills—English for them and Spanish for you. Language retention increases significantly during times of stress—those awkward moments when your mind is solely focused on interpreting what is being said.

Think about it—if culturally you were raised to avoid dissent, and *no* is not in your vocabulary when communicating with authority (high power distance behavior), there may be little else to convey beyond simply "Yes, OK."

To understand human behavior, one must understand power—who has it, how much they have, how they use it, and for what purpose. Different cultures interact with power differently, some viewing life as a zero-sum game, while others believe in working toward constant win–win scenarios. This often determines how competitive or cooperative cultures can be. Which is the subject of the next cultural dimension.

Dimension 3 :: Competitive versus Collaborative

"THE CRAB MENTALITY," HE SAID TO ME, catching me off guard as we exited the TEXO Latino Safety Superintendent Forum—a monthly safety meeting designed for Spanish-speaking workers in the Dallas–Fort Worth area, organized by the construction association TEXO.

"That's what you gotta look out for."

Marco Villasana, a safety coordinator at Azteca Construction, who was working at the Dallas–Fort Worth International Airport expansion in 2016, waited patiently as my face betrayed my confusion.

I quickly sifted through my mental filing cabinets for any content on crab cognition.

My search results came up empty.

Nada.

Feeling self-conscious, as if I should be aware of this so-called crab mentality, I attempted to save face.
I switched to Spanish.

"*¿La mentalidad de cangrejos?*" I said quizzically.

"*Sí. Exacto.*"
Yes. Exactly.

"Say you have a bucket full of crabs," Villasana explained. "As the ones closest to the top try to climb out to freedom, the other crabs, trying to get to the top themselves, pull them back down.

"It's a cultural thing I see all the time with Hispanics on the job. These guys survived a lot just to get here and they are very competitive—lots of machismo."

"Where do you see this combination of crab mentality and machismo on the job?" I asked.

"Training, coaching, safety," Villasana rattled off. "Everywhere. You need to look at the world from their perspective if you want to change their behavior."

Crabs or horses?

The third dimension we will cover is Competitive versus Collaborative. This dimension evaluates how different cultures view teamwork.

There are some individuals within a society who operate with a belief that life is a zero-sum game: The world has limited resources, and the outcomes are binary. In every interaction, one person wins and another loses.

Cultures operating with a competitive mind-set adhere to this life outlook. You might say people in these cultures live in a milder version of the 1985 film *Mad Max: Beyond Thunderdome.*

Two men enter.
One man leaves.

Yes, the crab mentality meshes well here.

On the opposite end of the spectrum, individuals from collaborative cultures believe there is always an opportunity for a win–win outcome. In every interaction, it is possible for both sides to get some version of what they want.

There's enough for everyone.
Let's work together.

Comedian Jerry Seinfeld has a great joke about racehorses and how if they were aware of the risks of getting injured on the track and what can happen as a result, they might be a bit more collaborative themselves.

I'll tell you the one thing the horses definitely do *not* know. They do not know that if you should accidentally trip and break your leg at any point during the race, we blow your brains out. I think they're missing that little tidbit of information. I think if they knew that, you'd see some mighty careful steppin' coming down the homestretch. "You win. I'll place. Whatever."

And then the punchline, as the horses discuss collaboration:

"It's all the same oatbag, fellas.
The important thing is your health."

This is the mentality of a highly collaborative culture. We could call this the "horse mentality."

There is plenty to go around.
Let's not kill ourselves here.

If we talk through exactly what it is each of us wants, surely we can find a reasonable agreement that works for everyone. This is the hallmark of a collaborative culture.

"Just win, baby."
Legendary Green Bay Packers football coach Vince Lombardi is lionized for his quote on winning: "Winning isn't everything; it's the only thing."[8]

Cited nearly as often is the three-word mantra from the late NFL Hall of Famer and Oakland Raiders owner Al Davis: "Just win, baby."

Yessir, we Americans are into winning. Geert Hofstede's research backed this up. Americans are more competitive than collaborative. However, many Hispanic countries are as well.

In fact, several countries are *more* competitive than the United States. I know. Hard to believe.

The collective reaction to this news that I typically get from Americans in *Good to Excelente* workshops is "What? No way." Then I ask how many people have either (1) spent time with people from these cultures or (2) spent time thinking about how different cultures work together.

Oftentimes never. It's tough to compare and contrast with a data set of 1.

So, revisiting Hofstede's factor-analysis scoring system, which countries have the most competitive cultures?

Most Competitive Countries

COUNTRY	SCORE
SLOVAKIA	110
JAPAN	95
HUNGARY	88
AUSTRIA	79
VENEZUELA	73

Somewhere in Slovakia right now a football (read: soccer) coach is scoffing at that tenderhearted softie Vince Lombardi.

And which countries have the most collaborative cultures? Sweden and Norway lead the way in looking for win–win scenarios, culturally speaking.

Most Collaborative Countries

COUNTRY	SCORE
SWEDEN	5
NORWAY	8
LATVIA	9
NETHERLANDS	14
DENMARK	16

Source: Hostede, et al

Now let's examine the Spanish-speaking countries at the core of this book, along with Uncle Sam.

Does anything jump out at you? What surprises you?

Let's quickly review four things that probably caught your eye.

U.S.A.: Fair to middling?
With a score of 62, Americans are just north of the mean score.

Slovakia and Japan are nearly 40 percent more competitive than we are?

Your patriotism may be kicking in right now, thinking of all the times we kicked both their asses in everything from Greco-Roman wrestling to world wars.

G2E Countries

COUNTRY	SCORE
VENEZUELA	73
MEXICO	69
COLOMBIA	64
ECUADOR	63
USA	**62**
PANAMA	44
EL SALVADOR	40
GUATEMALA	38
COSTA RICA	21

Source: Hostede, et al

But think back to the Power Distance Index for a minute. The United States is a lower power distance culture (with a score of 40). When it comes to thought and action, we embrace our independence. In the workplace, few of us enjoy working for an autocrat who determines every detail about what we do and how we do it.

We prefer an exchange of ideas with leadership and the freedom to complete a task based on the thoughts of the team responsible for getting it done.

That sounds like teamwork and collaboration. When it comes to competitive or collaborative behaviors, there are often multiple layers to consider. Observations don't always lead directly to insights. Some behaviors are difficult to understand, while others are fairly straightforward. One example of a competitive mind-set that is easier to identify is *machismo*.

Macho, macho man

"You, sir," I said, pointing to the twentysomething Hispanic in one of my cultural IQ workshops. "Can you explain to us gringos what *machismo* is?"

"Sure," he replied confidently. "It's just being a badass, bro. You challenge my manliness, I got no choice but to make a punk outta you. Take you out. That's machismo."

A silence settled over the group of 30 participants—then the room exploded into laughter. I did too.

"That's not the definition I typically use in corporate training," I admitted, laughing. "But how does this simpler definition sound? 'Machismo is characterized by male behavior that is very strong, aggressive, manly, and self-reliant.'"

"Yeah," the young man quipped. "That's what I said."

Machismo is an important factor in the competitive cultural mind-set in Hispanic countries. Hispanic countries are generally patriarchal, with male leadership exerting a disproportionately large share of influence. Among these men, to varying degrees to be sure, machismo behaviors can be observed often.

How does it affect behavior on the job?
Let's take a look at three examples.

1. Onboarding and training new hires

Given Hispanics' collectivist nature (remember Dimension 1: think large, cohesive groups), recruiting additional workers is often easy for companies that take care of their employees. So when openings at good companies become available, word spreads quickly among the network, the in-group.

When these new—often Spanish-speaking-only—
employees arrive, we typically outsource the onboarding
and new-hire training to the Spanish-speaking crews.
Well, we tell ourselves, *Jorge recruited him, and his
roofing crew speaks Spanish—they'll train him just fine.*

Maybe.
But maybe not.

Remember the crab mentality. Despite the inclusive,
collectivist nature that can make Hispanics more willing
to spread the good word on employment opportunities,
there remains a strong sense of competitiveness that is
still at play in this cultural group. Some members of the
team may feel threatened by new employees and could
deliberately withhold information, specific training, or
general job know-how.

Don't assume the new employee will become sufficiently
trained simply because his or her new teammates speak
Spanish and are familiar with one another.

2. Changing your coaching approach
In Dimension 1 in this chapter, Individualism versus
Collectivism, we discussed the concept of "losing face."
It might come as no surprise to learn that the flip side
of this coin—saving face—is strongly correlated with the
concept of machismo. We can safely assume that your
typical manly man probably doesn't want to look like
a fool in front of his peers.

Not that *any* of us ever want to look like fools, of course.
But as we know, different cultures handle things
differently. Their expectations are different. With
Hispanic cultures, which are often fuel-injected with
machismo, it's helpful for English-speaking leaders to be
more deliberate in their coaching and leadership tactics
so as to avoid causing Spanish speakers to lose face on
the job.

Recall from earlier the maxim my father told my brother and me: *praise in public, criticize in private*. That's good to keep in mind here as well. When problems arise with quality, safety, or communication, it is critical that leaders understand that the process of providing direct feedback to employees is not universal.

In individualistic cultures, like in the United States, the standard managerial technique is generally to confront problematic issues head on, face to face.

With Hispanic cultures, however, while it may seem counterintuitive, I have often found that *indirect* feedback is typically more effective.

Try leveraging the hierarchy within a Hispanic group to help deliver feedback. Quietly take aside the leader of the team (note: this would mean you'd have to know who the patriarch or leader of the group is) and openly discuss the shortcomings that you are noticing on the job. As the trusted head of the group, the leader will likely know the best course of action for relaying your message to the rest of the team—and eventually solving the problem. With this technique, you will be allowing the powerful collective group dynamics among Hispanics to self-regulate.

And more importantly, you'll have a better chance of avoiding unintentional insults that might otherwise limit your influence. There's an old adage that's pretty apt here: "People don't care how much you know until they know how much you care." Your ability to influence, persuade, and lead will be compromised if you are unintentionally insulting the people you work with when trying to give on-the-job feedback.

3. Keeping your workers safe

The day after Marco Villasana (the safety coordinator working at DFW Airport I mentioned earlier) shared the crab mentality with me, Ladd Henley, a bilingual safety manager at Capform Construction in Dallas, appeared as a guest on my podcast, *Red Angle Radio*. We spoke about machismo.

"It's one of the biggest barriers to safety that I deal with," he said, shaking his head. "Yesterday, I walked a guy to a cooling station because he appeared to be suffering from heat stress. Then I heard this phrase from some of the other workers:

¡OYE, VATO! ¿QUIERES QUE MI VIEJA LO HAGA?
Hey, dude! Want me to bring my old lady to do your job?

"They were just giving him shit," Ladd recounted. "They thought he was being lazy or trying to skip out on work, but he had all the classic signs of heat stress. It's that mentality [machismo] that gets people killed out here every summer."

When conducting your job hazard analysis, be sure to factor in the cultural aspects of machismo and how that may affect how workers behave—toward the work and toward one another.

Competitive crabs and collaborative horses
Managing people is far from easy. Personally speaking, it feels like herding cats sometimes. But whether your preferred analogy involves cats, crabs, horses, or any other species, your ability to change behavior and lead effectively will be in direct proportion to your willingness to adapt to the cultural paradigms of those you wish to lead.

The jobsite is a competitive place.
We know that.

Now we have a better sense of *how* competitive jobsites can be and how *that* influences the behavior of your workers. Now you can lead accordingly.

Dimension 4 :: Uncertainty Avoidance

"Hispanics love uncertainty," the weathered super-intendent said confidently, with a thick South Texas drawl.

"What makes you think that?" I asked.

"Well, take our concrete crews for example," he began. "You just point them in the right direction, and BAM!" He clapped his hands for dramatic affect. "They take off! If they weren't comfortable with uncertainty, I don't think we'd see them move so fast."

"OK. That makes sense," I admitted. "But how often do these concrete crews have rework?"

"Ahh, well, you know . . ." the superintendent sputtered as he massaged the bridge of his nose with his thumb and index finger. "Rework has been an issue. They sure are hard workers, but lately we've been doing everything twice . . . to do it right."

"That's no good," I said, obviously. "What if I told you Hispanic cultures, in general, are less comfortable with uncertainty than Anglos are. Do you think there could be a connection between uncertainty and rework?"

"Well, when you say it like that, I think there just might be."

Is different interesting? Or frightening?
For all the unique differences among cultures throughout the history of civilization, a common truth unites us all: the future is unknown to us. We're all aboard this train called life and where it leads—and when we and our family deboard—is a mystery.

Different cultures handle this transcendental mystery—uncertainty—in different ways. As Geert Hofstede notes, for some cultures uncertainty is a threat and is viewed with hostility. For other cultures, uncertainty is more of an exploration and is viewed with curiosity.

Regardless of cultural worldview, uncertainty is an emotion that is acquired and learned. No one is born with an innate preference toward uncertainty and ambiguity. "Uncertainty is shared throughout a culture and is reinforced within the family, school, and state."[9]

The fourth cultural dimension in this chapter, Uncertainty Avoidance, is defined "as the extent to which the members of a culture feel threatened by ambiguous or unknown situations."[10]

Understanding how different cultural groups grapple with uncertainty is important because uncertainty so often leads to anxiety, which can limit the effectiveness of people on the job. If people are anxious, they are likely to be distracted from the task at hand—precisely the conditions good leaders try to minimize. When workers are distracted and less focused on their objective, productivity decreases and the potential for injury increases.

Optimizing for uncertainty, then, has a direct impact on the bottom line. But this is hardly an easy task, is it? The challenge for any organization is to assemble a team and allow it to perform at its best, while still acknowledging that every person is unique and that individual behavior changes when working in groups. Team chemistry—or the lack thereof—influences how individuals behave. We may choose to perform a task one way when working by ourselves, only to completely change methodologies when two more colleagues are there to help us. With organizational options ranging from pure anarchy (*The only rule is there are no rules!*) to rigid bureaucracy (*Explicit rules are necessary due to incompetence and distrust!*), optimizing for uncertainty is not easy.

Furthermore, for many Anglo leaders learning about
Hispanics and their high uncertainty avoidance, the
research from Team Hofstede and others is
counterintuitive. Like the
Texas superintendent, our
intuition regarding
Hispanics' comfortability
with uncertainty is often
perfectly incorrect. For
many, it is the exact opposite
of what the research tells us
is true, that Hispanic cultures
wish to avoid uncertainty and
unstructured situations far
more than those from the
United States do.

Uncertainty Avoidance

COUNTRY	SCORE
GUATEMALA	101
EL SALVADOR	94
COSTA RICA	86
PANAMA	86
MEXICO	82
HONDURAS	50
USA	46

Source: Hostede, et al

Let's explore why that is, how
it affects the job, and what we
can do about it.

The table above shows six Hispanic countries, as
well as the United States, next to their Uncertainty
Avoidance scores per Hofstede's system of scoring. The
higher the score a culture has, the more that culture
wishes to eliminate or avoid uncertainty.

Looking at this list, the first thing you should notice is the
range of scores among countries in close proximity to one
another. Guatemala and Honduras, while they share a
border, have very different levels of comfortability with
unstructured situations. Guatemalans are twice as likely
to desire to limit the uncertainty in their environment
compared to Hondurans.

Comparatively, the culture in the United States is far
more comfortable with ambiguity than our neighbor to the
south, Mexico, is. Two questions emerge here: Why is
there ambiguity in your business operations? How can we
reduce it to improve performance?

"There are no dumb questions . . ." and other cultural clichés

One surefire way to reduce ambiguity is to ask questions. However, as we learned with the Power Distance Index, different cultures view authority differently, so asking questions is sometimes not so easy to do. While citizens of the United States are, as a culture, more comfortable questioning authority, people of Hispanic cultures are typically much less likely to do so, not wanting to be seen as being disrespectful.

When an Anglo manager delivers instructions on a jobsite, for example, his Hispanic team will generally listen. The team members may or may not fully understand the instructions, but they will listen. Interrupting to ask questions, again, may be perceived as being disrespectful. And admitting that they don't understand (either the instructions or the language) could cause them to lose face in front of their peers.

Are you beginning to sense the challenge here?

Members of Hispanic cultures typically want to eliminate as much uncertainty as possible. But they are also not generally inclined to engage in the kind of direct dialogue (asking probing questions, for example) that would eliminate the very uncertainty they are trying to avoid.

Hispanics' high Uncertainty Avoidance scores coupled with their high Power Distance Index scores sets the table for confusion. Sprinkle in the language barrier and you have a recipe for miscommunication, rework, and potential injury.

The graph below plots both the Uncertainty Avoidance and the Power Distance Index dimensions. As with the graph earlier plotting Individualism versus Collectivism and the Power Distance Index, the United States maintains a noticeable spatial distance from its Hispanic counterparts.

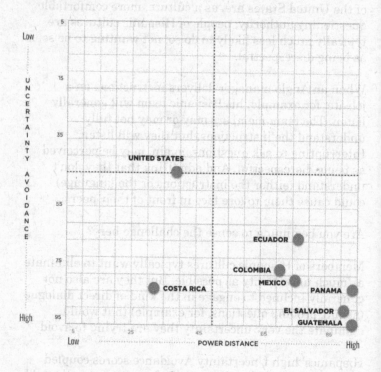

V.A.R.K.: How to reduce uncertainty

Albert Einstein is often quoted as having defined insanity as doing the same thing over and over again and expecting different results.

This happens frequently on the jobsite. Even after a problem has been identified, too many managers will repeatedly round up their crews and say, "OK. We're gonna go over this one . . . more . . . time."

Let's try some different tactics.
Let's choose sanity.

Reducing uncertainty, at its core, is about teaching and learning. As discussed throughout this book, sometimes we need to adjust our teaching method depending on who the student is and how he or she learns.

So, how *do* people learn? And how can we use that knowledge to reduce uncertainty in learning situations—that is, on the job?

Human beings learn in different ways. Four, to be exact—visual, auditory, read–write, and kinesthetic.

The first three in this list are more or less self-explanatory. Some people learn better with visuals, others learn better by listening, and some learn better by reading and writing.

The last one might not be as familiar to you.

Kinesthetic comes from the word *kinesiology*, which is the study of how the body moves. When you see the word *kinesthetic*, think of *doing*. Kinesthetic learners prefer hands-on activities, situations where they are physically engaged in the process of learning.

I, along with a broad segment of the population, am a visual learner (hence all the photos, images, charts, and graphs in this book). I recommend the acronym V.A.R.K. to consider the various learning modalities to help reduce uncertainty.

- **V**isual
- **A**udio
- **R**ead–Write
- **K**inesthetic

To help your message reach the largest number of people, refer to V.A.R.K as a checklist. In addition to your verbal instructions (which would be *A* in the V.A.R.K acronym— *A* for *Audio*), try factoring in the following ideas to deliver your message more effectively.

Make a checklist

In *The Checklist Manifesto*, author Dr. Atul Gawande extolls the virtues of the common checklist better than I ever could:

> [W]e need a different strategy for overcoming failure, one that builds on experience and takes advantage of the knowledge people have but somehow also makes up for our inevitable human inadequacies. And there is such a strategy—though it will seem almost ridiculous in its simplicity, maybe even crazy to those of us who have spent years carefully developing ever more advanced skills and technologies. It is a checklist.

A Red Angle client once told me of a surprising improvement she witnessed when two minor changes were made to their daily job hazard analysis (JHA). First, it was simplified from 50 general things to the *15* most common hazards on the job witnessed daily. The team applied the 80/20 rule and kept it simple. And then their bilingual foreman translated it into Spanish and reviewed it with the crew for understanding.

These two seemingly minor changes resulted in immediate compliance improvement.

Checklists work.

V.A.R.K. checklist for the Job Hazard Analysis (JHA)
Verbal instructions = Audio
Spanish language JHA = Read

Here are a few other ideas to increase the probability of your message getting through.

A picture (on an iPad) is worth a thousand words. . .
An iPad or any tablet computer is large enough to show
several people at once what it is you are talking about.
Use it to show a photo or use one of the many whiteboard
apps currently available.

Or . . . use an actual whiteboard.
Not as practical. But rework, by definition, isn't either.

V.A.R.K. checklist for a whiteboard
Image = Visual
Verbal instructions = Audio

People like videos
The smartphone in your pocket right now has incredible
screen resolution. Use it to create brief videos of repetitive
tasks or processes that have been problematic in the past.
When miscommunication leads to rework that could be
prevented in the future, create a brief video. Remember,
history repeats itself—unless you do something about it.

Follow these steps to change the future:

1. *Hold the phone sideways.*
2. *Video record the proper execution. (Keep it brief, Scorsese!)*
3. *Save the video to your own digital library on your
   company's intranet.*
4. *Share it with your team.*

Video *en español*
Once you have your video, record a voiceover in Spanish.
(I recommend investing in a decent microphone for these
recordings. I've been using the Yeti Blue microphone,
which retails for around $100, for desktop audio recording
for the past few years. It's durable, inexpensive, and looks
cool sitting on your desk.)

V.A.R.K. checklist for video recording
Video = Visual
Audio (in video, in language of preference) = Audio
Verbal instructions = Audio

Note: Consider adding text graphics for your audience to read on top of the video for additional emphasis.

Audio *en español*
Using the voice recorder app on your smartphone, ask a trusted bilingual colleague to translate your message ahead of time. Note: You'll have to think through the amplification required depending on your jobsite. Your smartphone's speakers may be fine for a group of 5, but for a group of 20, you might need some decent speakers.

V.A.R.K. checklist for audio recording
Verbal instructions = Audio

Seeing is believing—*doing* is even better
Sometimes the most effective way to eliminate any confusion or uncertainty when teaching someone something is to have the person physically perform the activity. This is where the *K* in V.A.R.K. comes into play: *kinesthetic*—remember, think of *doing*.

For example, if you are hosting a training session on how to wear a safety harness properly, you can avoid a lot of uncertainty simply by having attendees perform the actual steps of putting one on themselves.

I've attended multiple sessions like this over the past few years where, due to time constraints, attendees were not able to physically demonstrate their understanding of the proper technique.

And yet we are surprised when OSHA reports that Hispanics are disproportionately more likely to be injured or killed on the job—the most common injury being a fall from heights.[11]

Yes, it may take more time to have several members of a group fumble their way through a fit test for a safety harness, but sometimes that's the best way to learn. And it requires significantly less time than your company's post-injury procedure, I assure you.

V.A.R.K. checklist for group practice
Acting out behavior = Visual (for the group)
Acting out behavior = Kinesthetic
Verbal instructions = Audio

Note: While this demonstration is underway, a manager can be recording it with his smartphone for future training as a video.

Mix and match
With minimal effort, you can include multiple items on the V.A.R.K. checklist. Continue delivering your verbal instructions (Audio) and include an image or brief video using your tablet or smartphone (Visual).

Distribute a Spanish-language job hazard analysis that, ideally, includes images, icons, or graphics (Read, Visual); and, if applicable, have a few members of the group perform the activity live (Kinesthetic).

This process will help reduce uncertainty. During the training, provide positive reinforcement with a few small Spanish phrases you may already know:

Muy bien	(**MOOH**-ee bee-**AYN**)	very good
Otra vez	(**OH**-trah **BAYS**)	again
Excelente	(ayk-say-**LAYN**-tay)	excellent
Mejor	(may-**HOHR**)	better
Gracias	(**GRAH**-see-ahs)	thank you

Certainly uncertain

Certainty drives consistency and confidence. Instead of assuming how people feel, tap into multiple ways of communicating your message. Assume less, observe more.

Think of a recent example of rework on your jobsite or some frustration you've had with some of your Hispanic workers. Did you immediately assume the challenge they were having was the result of a lack of cognitive ability or language comprehension?

The challenge could also be a cultural barrier. Or potentially all three.

As a leader, it is your responsibility to adjust your management style to meet the needs of those you lead.

So, could there be a connection between uncertainty and rework?

Remember the words of the superintendent from South Texas: "Well, when you say it like that, I think there just might be."

Dimension 5 :: Trust

I WASN'T INTERESTED IN HEARING JUNIOR SPEAK. I didn't trust that his time—my time, really—on stage was worth it. Listen to his father? Gladly. But not Junior.

It was April 15, 2016. I was in Provo, Utah, at the Associated Schools of Construction (ASC) Management annual conference. Along with Professor James Jenkins of Purdue University, I was presenting a research paper on our "Safety Spanish" collaboration.

The keynote speaker for the Day 1 lunch was Stephen M. R. Covey, the son of Stephen Covey, author of *The 7 Habits of Highly Effective People*.

Apparently Covey the Younger wrote a book about something.[12] But I wasn't interested in hearing him speak.

Within 30 seconds, I became interested. The *something* Covey was speaking to us about was *trust*.

He revealed a pair of equations for trust in relationships. This was the first:

$$\textit{When Trust is Low = Speed} \downarrow \textit{+ Cost} \uparrow$$

When you don't trust someone, the speed of business slows down. Without trust, you cannot move forward with the confidence that, if things turn for the worst, we will work together collaboratively to find a mutually beneficial solution.

Without trust, you spend time ensuring you *CYA*: cover your, um, interests, because the other party surely isn't.

As a former estimator, I experienced firsthand how a lack of information can lead to higher costs. Whether it's poorly written specifications or incorrect plans, uncertainty leads to a lack of trust. If there is a lack of trust in what is being built and how, then the risk that something will go wrong increases. And this increased risk can lead to rework, which results in higher prices.

Covering your ass takes time—and time is money. Covey called this a "distrust tax."

The distrust tax is extra investment of time and money required to conduct business in low-trust relationships. Low-trust relationships are, as Covey said, "an economic decision resulting in higher prices."

Now consider the corollary:

When Trust is High = Speed ↑ + Cost ↓

When you trust someone completely, the speed of business accelerates: You don't waste additional time scrutinizing the worst-case scenario. And you know that if things go off the rails, you will work it out with your trusted partner.

Risk is reduced. You trust your partner to treat you the same way your partner would treat him or herself.

Covey summarized his threefold message:
- *Trust is an economic decision.*
- *Trust is also a leadership decision.*
- *Trust is a learnable competency.*

"You should have a bias for trust," Covey advised.

Scanning the faces at my table in Provo at the ASC conference, I realized this message of trust would be harder to accept for some than for others. Our table, mirroring the professorial audience as a whole, was diverse. There were two Anglos, a Nigerian, an Indian (from Bangalore), an Irishman (from Dublin), one Chinese person, one educator from Puerto Rico, and me, a ginger from Chicago.

To varying degrees, Covey's message would be perceived differently because different cultures have different baseline levels of trust.

How much do you trust me?
When we talk about cultural trust in Red Angle workshops, I always ask the group this question: "On a scale from 1 to 10, how much do you trust me?

"A score of 10 would indicate total trust," I say, explaining the boundaries of this exercise. "You'd loan me your debit card and pin number without a second thought, confident that I would not betray your trust.

"A score of 1 would indicate that not only do you *not trust* me, you'd expect me to physically injure you during our time together today."

Then I begin asking people directly.
"What trust score do you give me?"

I have received my highest trust scores in Minnesota. Nearly all 7s, 8s, and 9s, as well as my only 10. "Gimme your debit card now!" I remember demanding. "And your 4-digit pin. Let's play this out!"

When I told one workshop group in Minneapolis that these scores were absurdly high for this exercise, a middle-aged man sitting in the front shrugged sheepishly. "Minnesotans," he said, sighing, "are very trusting people."

In New Jersey, however, the scores participants gave me were much lower. Nearly all 2s, 3s, and 4s, with my only 1. Ever. "Wait!" I'd said to them, stunned. "You actually think I'm going to hurt you? Why? Because gingers have bad tempers?"

When I asked a Jersey Shore twentysomething why he gave me a 2, he responded firmly. "I don't f****** know you, bro."

Fair enough.

Different cultures—from a macro-perspective of a single country, down to a submarket within a single city—have different baseline levels of trust.

No "trust" in Spanish

In the Spanish language, there is no direct translation for the word "trust." The word *confianza* is as close as we get.

Does *confianza* look familiar to you?

CONFIANZA
(kohn-fee-**AHN**-sah)

It looks similar to *confidence*, right?
That's what it means, confidence.
And trust.

Language reflects the culture from which it comes.
In Hispanic cultures, the two concepts of *confidence* and *trust* are inextricably linked.

In *The Culture Map: Breaking Through the Invisible Boundaries of Global* Business,[13] author Erin Meyer explains that trust has two components: cognitive and affective.

Cognitive trust relates to the head. It's an analysis of the skills a person or an organization has. **Affective**

trust goes to the heart—it's emotional. It's the trust you *feel*.

As we discussed in Dimension 1, Americans are generally individualistic.

Citizens of the United States value freedom, independence, and flexibility—especially in the workplace. As a culture, we tend to separate the personal from the professional. Hispanics are more collective in nature, and the relationships among those in their in-group, as well as those outside it, extend beyond the invisible barrier that separates our *work life* from our *home life*.

When thinking of these cultural differences regarding trust, I'm reminded of the classic 1996 film *Jerry Maguire*. The part that resonated most with me was not the now-famous line "Show me the money!" Rather, it was a quote from the character Bob Sugar about the difference between friends and business. Before we get to that, let me set the scene for you . . .

On a rainy night, in a surge of emotion, Jerry, played by Tom Cruise, drafts his vision statement for the SMI sports agency, his employer. Here is a writer/director Cameron Crowe's script:

JERRY'S VOICE
What started out as one page became twenty-five. Suddenly I was my father's son. I was remembering the simple pleasures of this job, how I ended up here out of law school, the way a stadium sounds when one of my players performs well on the field . . . I was remembering even the words of the late Dicky Fox, the original sports agent who said:

DICKY FOX
The key to this job is personal relationships.

As Jerry continues typing, his voice is excited now.

JERRY'S VOICE
And suddenly it was all pretty clear. The answer was fewer clients. Caring for them, caring for ourselves, and the games too. Starting our lives, really.

In the film, Jerry espouses a return to the fundamentals of representation—truly caring for each client. He says something strikingly un-capitalistic, un-American: "The answer was fewer clients. Less money. Caring for them, caring for ourselves . . ."

What Jerry is talking about here is *affective trust*. He's speaking from the heart, not the head. Which is why after distributing 110 copies of his vision statement to his firm, he has second thoughts.

His head knows the phrase "fewer clients, less money" will be problematic.

A few scenes later, Maguire's mentee, Bob Sugar, asks to meet for lunch at a busy diner. Sugar fires him. From there, a race ensues as Jerry and Bob (as a representative of SMI) attempt to secure the loyalty of their clients, who now have a choice to make about their representation.

Bob Sugar, speaking to one client, cuts to the chase with the following line, which I find so memorable and which I think articulates how different cultures think about trust:

> "Are you in or are you out?
> It's not show friends, it's show business."

These are the two types of trust writ large.
Bob Sugar is the personification of *cognitive trust*.
He candidly separates relationships and business.
He believes his role is to make his firm money by making his clients money.

That's it.
It's business, not personal.

Jerry Maguire, on the other hand, embodies *affective trust*. His mentor, Dicky Fox, said it succinctly: "The key to this business is personal relationships."

Fox and Maguire believe friendship will, in time, ultimately deliver more revenue.

These are two approaches to trust. Now let's see how that directly relates to culture and your Hispanic workforce.

In *The Culture Map*, Meyer says these two cultural approaches to trust are manifested in a preference for either task-based (cognitive) or relationship-based (affective) trust.

Meyer defines task-based trust like this:

> *Trust is built through business-related activities. Work relationships are built and dropped easily, based on the practicality of the situation. You do good work consistently, you are reliable, I enjoy working with you, I trust you.*

Does this feel about right to you?
Is this how you identify with trust on the job?

Americans, Meyer (a trusting Minnesotan herself) writes, are anchored in task-based waters.

During the Great Recession, numerous contractors with decades-long histories of partnership were cast aside as they were unable to meet the pricing or manpower needs at the time.

Working in the estimating department for a construction firm, I frequently heard statements about subcontractors like the following: "We don't have to like them to contract them. If we believe they will perform well and their pricing is great, sign the contract."

It's not show friends, it's show business.

Mexico is on the opposite end of the spectrum, firmly entrenched in relationship-based trust. Here is Meyer's description:

> *Trust is built through sharing meals, evening drinks, and visits at the coffee machine. Work relationships build up slowly over the long term. I've seen who you are at a deep level, I've shared personal time with you, I know others well who trust you, I trust you.*

You're probably noticing a pattern here. The United States on one end, Mexico and other Hispanic countries on the other.

Neither is better than the other.
Just different.

TRUST

U.S.A.   MEXICO

Task-based   Relationship-based
Cognitive Trust   Affective Trust

Source: Erin Meyer, The Culture Map

Build trust on the job

Time is money . . . and we're always a little short on both. Relationship building can be terribly inefficient—it takes time. But in the long term, it can have a great return on investment. To get more of what you want (without totally abandoning our American, task-based nature), consider a few specific ways to lean more toward relationship-based trust and get to know your workers.

Identify language of preference

Whenever you are hiring, onboarding, or training anyone, you should always learn the individual's language of preference. Pose the following question—in writing—in both English and Spanish and have the individual check the preferred box.

We are going to show you a video that will help save your life, and then we will test you on it afterward. Do you prefer the video be in English or Spanish?

Identify cultural context

By this point in the book, you have (hopefully) significantly improved your understanding of the cultural nuances that can affect job performance. A simple way to transfer this knowledge into action is by understanding the Hispanic individuals on your job. Namely, is the person native or foreign-born?

If the person was born in the United States, his or her cultural leanings will be far more "American" and task-based than an individual born somewhere else. The next obvious question is how recently the person arrived in the United States.

A craft worker who was working on a ranch in northern Mexico 30 days ago will think and act differently than someone who arrived from Mexico City 30 years ago.

Ask the individual about his or her goals—about what is important to him or her. If you aren't interested in your employees in the long term, how can you expect them to be interested in your company in the long term?

What's In It For Me?

Adjust the dial to WII-FM: What's In It For Me?
Amidst the current labor shortage in the construction and
manufacturing industries, a common complaint I hear is
that the efforts made to connect with Hispanic workers
are often fruitless. After all, why bother with improvements to language or cultural intelligence when Hispanic
craft workers will jump ship when your competitor offers
them 75 cents more an hour? Fair question.

Tune into WII-FM and consider what we know so far
about the individuals. From previous sections in this
book, we've learned about how recently Hispanics have
arrived in the United States and what their goals are—
at least in a broad sense. If 80 percent of a worker's
weekly paycheck is being sent to his family abroad as a
remittance, then hourly wage may be the most important
factor in retaining him.

More money, however, is not the most important goal for
every employee. In *Drive: The Surprising Truths about
What Motivates Us*, author Daniel Pink notes that money
is a determining factor only *up to certain threshold*. Once
that threshold is reached ("I need to make $25/hour" or
"I need to be able to say I make six figures"), other factors
weigh far more heavily on the career decisions people
make—where they choose to work, how long they stay
there, and what may cause them to look for employment
elsewhere.

For Hispanic craft workers, WII-FM is a question of roots.
Do they have roots established in their local community?
Are their roots back in their country of origin?

Are their roots in some other city in the United States?

If a worker has family in the local community—a house, 3.5 kids, etc.—the threshold theory of salary will apply more uniformly. Money will be important up to a point. Then other factors such as job security and proximity to work will start to become more of a priority.

For workers with roots in another city, whether that may be in Guatemala or Los Gatos, California, it's more likely to be *Jerry Maguire* time: "Show me the money!"

Hispanics, we know, are predominantly collectivists and, as such, have a strong sense of family. For many foreign-born Hispanics, their sole focus is often to work to provide cash for their family. Hispanics send billions of dollars of remittances back to their home countries.[14]

If remittances are the primary motivation for a large portion of your foreign-born workforce, then, yes, an increase in pay will be attractive. More money means more money to send home.

Something else to consider is the reality that many Hispanic workers leverage less-than-reputable banking services to cash their checks or wire money to their family, and these services often can come with steep fees. Thinking outside the box, can you provide information or banking options for your employees to ensure only minimum fees are tacked on to their hard-earned money sent home—wherever that may be?

Spending time getting to know Hispanic employees, tuning into WII-FM, and then actively trying to help them is how to build trust. And trust is always a sound economic decision.

When Trust is High = Speed ↑ + Cost ↓

Dimension 6 :: Persuasion

"DON'T TELL ME ABOUT THE BIRTHING PAINS, HARTMANN—just show me the baby."

The comment from the division president at my company back in 2005 caught me off guard.

I'd been told we would have 45 minutes to present the details of a new project we were about to begin. And now, two minutes into my carefully prepared slide deck, I was being told to cut to the chase.

"We trust you and your team," said the president. "That's why you're leading it. Jump to the slides that talk about the primary challenges, how you'll overcome them, and then walk us through your financials."

I'll get there, I thought to myself, *but the context and nuances about how we arrived at those conclusions are important, right?*

Reading my thoughts with alarming accuracy, the president continued, "I'm less concerned about the context and nuances and more about your *conclusions*. You've got the entire executive team here; just give us the summary."

Executive . . . summary.
Aha. Got it.

Jumping ahead to slide number 88, I explained the primary project risks, how the team was planning for them, and how much money we planned to return to the business. A rapid-fire Q&A session followed.

Ten minutes later, the meeting was over.
The executives filed out of the room quickly, quietly.

"Don't tell me about the birthing pains—just show me the baby."

This very culturally American directive has stayed with me to this day and continues to influence how I write, edit, and present information. It's a great exercise in focusing on efficiency and a perfect example of the MED (minimum effective dose) in action: the bare minimum amount of context and insight to deliver the maximum results. Nothing more.

Time is money.
Cut to the chase.
KISS: Keep It Simple Stupid.
Start with the executive summary.
No paragraphs, bullet points only.
Just show me the baby.

It's important to note here that this idea of brevity and efficiency when conveying information is not a globally shared mentality. Sure, it's very American, but as we have seen time and time again, just because something is American doesn't make it universal. This is crucial to keep in mind when considering your Hispanic workforce and the techniques you use to teach and manage them.

As author Erin Meyer explains, different cultures are persuaded in different ways depending on how they process information.

Some cultures prefer to have the fundamental principles of an argument come first, followed by the conclusion— what she calls *principles-first persuasion*. Begin at the beginning, end at the end.

That kind of process made sense to me when I'd been carefully crafting my slide deck for the executive team. I'd wanted to give them all the information first so that they were fully prepared for when I ended with the results. But that wasn't what they wanted.

Indeed, other cultures, like many Americans (including my president), prefer that the conclusion comes *first*, followed by elements of the argument in descending order, with the most important near the top, what Meyer calls ***applications-first persuasion***. Start with the end, then support it with the beginning.

This is what my president had wanted: persuade with the crucial information first, then go into detail to show how it all fits together.

Meyer describes each persuasion type in the following way:

Principles-first
Individuals have been trained to first develop the theory or complex concept before stating a fact, statement, or opinion. The preference is to begin a message or report by building up a theoretical argument before moving on to a conclusion. The conceptual principles underlying each situation are valued.

Applications-first
Individuals are trained to begin with a fact, statement, or opinion and later add concepts to back up or explain the conclusion as necessary. The preference is to begin a message or report with an executive summary or bullet points. Discussions are approached in a practical, concrete manner. Theoretical or philosophical discussions are avoided in a business environment.

As the graphic that follows shows, Uncle Sam is indeed persuaded more by seeing the newborn than by hearing about the delivery saga. Mexico, the only Hispanic country included in Meyer's research, is in the middle, favoring neither application- nor principles-first persuasion.

PERSUASION

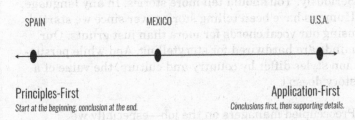

SPAIN   MEXICO   U.S.A.

Principles-First
Start at the beginning, conclusion at the end.

Application-First
Conclusions first, then supporting details.

Source: Erin Meyer, The Culture Map

The practicalities of persuasion

Now that we have a better sense of how different cultures respond to different methods of persuasion, how can we adjust our styles to connect more effectively with our Hispanic workers?

The good news is you don't need any wholesale changes. Like any good leader does, consider your audience. When providing directives about job hazards and the changes needed to stay safe, for example, keep in mind that your group of English-speaking superintendents may not need too much additional information to be persuaded. They are more likely to be motivated with applications-first info—how it applies to them and what they need to do.

What about the Spanish-speaking group being led by the bilingual foreman?

They may be persuaded more by principles-first information—what happened and how these directives came about. They may be looking for more context.

Encourage the bilingual foreman to share some details about the backstory and why the jobsite is now implementing these changes. Ask him to provide a bit more detail than he normally would to a group of English-speakers.

Tell stories

Seriously. You should tell more stories. In any language. Humans have been telling stories ever since we started using our vocal chords for more than just grunts. Our minds are hardwired for storytelling. And while persuasion styles differ by country and culture, the value of a story doesn't.

Preoccupied managers on the job—especially we Americans—often communicate with short bursts of directives, typically excluding the contextual details of why something needs to get done.

Those details are important for everyone, though. And they are especially important for principles-first cultures.

Stories don't have to be long. Actually, the simpler the better—simple stories are persuasive stories.

Whether we're trying to persuade and influence our spouse, our kids, our boss, or a Hispanic craft worker on our jobsite, our ability to lead depends on our ability to persuade.

Consider your audience and where they likely fall on the line from principles-first to applications-first persuasion.

For example, in 2016 a commercial general contractor contacted Red Angle about improving retention among its Hispanic craft workers. Workers, the CEO told me, often left the company for slight wage increases.

The high rate of turnover was frustrating the CEO. He felt his company had an attractive ESOP (employee stock ownership plan) that was demonstrably better than the competition's benefits plans. If this were true, though, then why were employees leaving for 50 cents more per hour?

We reviewed the cultural concept of principles-first and applications-first persuasion with the executive team. Then we examined their operational process to recruit, hire, and on-board Hispanic craft workers. That's when the CEO realized something.

"Is it possible we're not communicating a principles-first view of our company with Hispanic employees?" he asked. "The video that talks about the ESOP is two minutes long and it's only available in English. We mention the ESOP briefly, assuming everyone knows how important it is. Then we list a few bullet points. That's it. Same thing with our benefits package. I think we're using the same message to two different audiences and ultimately not communicating well enough to our Hispanic workers."

After a slight pause, the CEO asked the following question: "What if we shared more of the backstory—the underlying principles of our ESOP and why it's valuable to them—and better explained their potential gains by staying with us in the long term?"

Running with that idea, the company shifted gears and tried for more of a principles-first approach. Within a few months, they had updated their process of recruiting, hiring, and onboarding Hispanic craft workers to include the story behind the ESOP—how it happened, why it happened, and how it serves the long-term interests of the company's employees.

The superior benefits package was explained through first-person testimonials from Hispanic employees on video. Following the video, Spanish-speaking employees from Human Resources answered questions and were available to help the craft workers complete their benefits paperwork.

Six months following the implementation of this new process, the results were positive. Applications among Hispanic craft workers for benefits increased 30 percent.

Month-over-month turnover compared to the previous year was down 15 percent. The problem wasn't gone completely, but the company was trending in the right direction.

Dimension 7 :: Universalism versus Particularism

STEVE CALLED IN A PANIC. He skipped the pleasantries and launched right into what was rocking his world at the moment.

"We had an accident out here. We're trying to figure out exactly what happened—we're not getting very far. Can you come out here now?"

Steve, the safety director at a Red Angle client, explained the severity of the injuries that had just befallen two craft workers. They had been working from a boom lift when, for reasons yet to be determined, it fell over.

A dozen Hispanic workers had been in the area and had witnessed the accident. These men had all been quarantined and were being interviewed by other members of the safety team. Nearly all required a translator.

Two hours later, I met Steve on the job.
He was visibly frustrated.

"None of these guys will talk. None of 'em say they saw anything! We may have a fatality on our hands here, and these guys—who were all within 100 feet of the accident—won't give us any details."

He paused, mentally sifting through options.

"Will you interview these guys and see if you can get any more information from them?"

I told Steve my efforts would probably provide little value at this point. "Whaddya mean?" Steve demanded to know. "Isn't this your thing—the culture and communication deal?"

I tried to explain to Steve that everyone is likely very distressed by the traumatic event that just occurred. Emotions of fear and guilt would be running high among the Hispanic craft workers present at the time of the accident.

"I get that," Steve said, "but by withholding information, they are interfering with the investigation."

"Mentally, these workers are operating in survival mode right now," I told Steve. "In this state, they are relying on the oldest, most fundamental truths they were raised with. While this situation may seem black and white for you, there's a lot of gray here for them."

Steve stared at me, confused and a little annoyed. He was hoping for a simple solution for his information-gathering problem. Instead, I asked if we could sit down somewhere so I could introduce him to the cultural dimension of Universalism versus Particularism.

Fifty shades of *gris*
Some people see the world as ruled by simple truths—a universal code of conduct—that are either black or white. There is no *gris* (**GREES**), or "gray," area.

Stealing is always bad.

Yep, even if you have starving children at home.
It's black and white.
Don't make it harder than it needs to be.

Lying is wrong.

Yep, even if it's a white lie and you're protecting a friend. It's black and white. Don't look for an angle you can rationalize yourself into believing.

This standard of evaluating behavior is known as universalism. There is a universal code of conduct for all situations. The situational context isn't important.

It's either right or wrong.
It's either black or white.
It's universal.

Culture in the United States is often universal. There is one set of rules and it applies to everyone. Given the tempestuous split from an English monarchy that abused its power, it is unsurprising that young America opted for more of a universal perspective. Universalism is an anti-monarchical view of the world.

Universalism is also more efficient—it allows us to focus more on the task, regardless of the relationship. Universalists don't get hung up on the details. Uncle Sam is a universalist.

Hispanics, on the other hand, lean more toward particularism. With particularism, the details matter. These particulars provide the situational context, which greatly determines behavior in certain situations.

In Red Angle workshops, I like to play out these two mind-sets by borrowing an example from author and social scientist Dr. David Livermore.

Pretend you are a passenger in a friend's car and you are driving along a winding road. Your friend is speeding and accidentally hits someone crossing the road.

The police arrive later and begin to interrogate. Do you protect your friend? Do you cover for him and say the pedestrian came out of nowhere? Or do you simply say, "Yes, officer. He was speeding. And we hit that person crossing the road."

The responses I often hear reveal a lot about how different cultures apply different codes of conduct.

The Anglos in the workshop frequently begin by asking a few questions.

Did the crosser die?
How fast was the car actually going?
Was this taking place at night?

Then they most often arrive at this answer: *I'd tell the truth.*

My friend was speeding and he hit someone. He must own that now. I'm not going to lie for him. It is black and white.

Commit the crime . . . do the time.

Anglos typically apply a universal code of conduct to the situation.

Presented with the same scenario, Hispanics and many other particularist cultures see things a bit differently. They see a scenario with many shades of gray, specifically with respect to the relationship between the passenger and the driver.

"Particularist cultures believe we have special obligations to people we know," writes Livermore. "Particularist judgments focus on the exceptional nature of present circumstances."[15]

Hispanics, too, begin by asking some questions.

How well do I know the driver?
Is he family?
Is he a friend of a friend?
Or is he some random Uber driver?

In the workshop, I disclose to the participants that the driver is not a blood relative, but rather a close friend. And that makes the decision easy.

"Of course I'd cover for him—he's a close friend," says one participant.

"I wouldn't outright lie, but I'd be vague in my recollection," says another.

Livermore cuts to the chase: "What's fair? Applying one rule equally to everyone, or accounting for unusual circumstances?"

For Hispanics, applying one universal rule for everyone makes little sense. Of course you should treat family differently (think large, extended families that share a collectivist mind-set). They *are* different—they're family!

Applying universalist or particularist codes of conduct extend beyond hypotheticals among family and friends; they are clearly present in commerce as well.

When you visited the *tiendas* ("stores") on the outskirts of Cancún, shopping for an onyx bull for your mantle back home in the States, did you notice there was no sale price listed? Why is that? Do you think you'd be offered a different price than a local?

Of course.

You assume a local would get a lower price than some rich *estadounidense* ("American") staying at the all-inclusive hotel a few miles away. This is particularism.

After haggling with the shopkeeper for 30 minutes, you purchase the onyx bull for 900 pesos (around $50). Money changes hands. You are happy. Then a local saunters in and buys an identical onyx bull for 250 pesos. You are now unhappy. "Unfair!" you scream.

A price for one should be the price for all.
This is the basic tenet of universalism.

You may see the world through a lens of black and white, right and wrong. Your culture has nurtured this perspective. Others see many shades of gray. Neither is better than the other, just different.

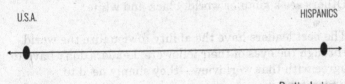

U.S.A.   HISPANICS

Universalism
One set of universal rules;
black and white.

Particularism
The particular details of a
situation affect my view of it.

Source: Dr. David Livermore, *Leading with Cultural Intelligence*

An array of many colors

Steve, always blunt, told me how he felt with a sarcastic chuckle. "Well, Hartmann, you weren't much help at all. Other than telling me I am a . . . what did you call it? Master of the Universe?"

Steve had been to my cultural-intelligence workshop and completed Red Angle's six-week course on Safety Spanish. I considered him a friend, so I was blunt with him.

"Look, Steve. You take safety very seriously and, obviously, that's important. But if you don't actively develop trust with these Hispanic craft workers in what you say and do . . . and if you're more focused on eliminating tasks on your to-do list than building relationships . . . and if you refer to *them* and *they*, instead of *us* and *we* . . . you cannot be surprised with their lack of engagement here. For these employees who just witnessed a tragedy involving two of their friends, you are not a person of particular interest here. They respect your position, sure, but that's about it."

Different cultures view the world through different colored lenses.

Some have an array of many colors, through which each situation is saturated differently, according to the particular elements in play.

Others see a simpler world, black and white.

The best leaders have the ability to visualize the world through the eyes of their followers. Leaders don't have to agree with that worldview—they simply need to understand it.

Dimension 8 :: Being versus Doing

I PLAYED COLLEGE FOOTBALL FOR TWO YEARS (rather unsuccessfully, I might add) at Eastern Illinois University. I made it on the playing field just once, quarterbacking the second half of a blowout. I threw one incompletion and broke one wrist. On the same play.

My lone highlight from EIU was hosting former Dallas Cowboys quarterback Tony Romo's recruiting visit. This has allowed me to say that, technically speaking, I stepped aside to enable Tony's wonderful collegiate and eventual NFL career.[16]

I'm sure Tony feels the same.

More so than my fumbled football dreams, I remember this quirky sandwich joint nearby called Jimmy John's. Now a ubiquitous fast-food eatery, back in 1996 there weren't many stores, and the very first one was in Charleston, Illinois, 100 yards from my TV-repair-shop-turned-apartment.

On one of the walls at Jimmy John's was a somewhat random panoply of signs hanging all over the place. One in particular caught my eye. It told the tale of a Mexican fisherman and a Harvard MBA and was titled *How Much Is Enough?*

> *The American investment banker was at the pier of a small coastal Mexican village when a small boat with just one fisherman docked. Inside the small boat were several large-fin tuna. The American complimented the Mexican on the quality of his fish and asked how long it took to catch them.*
>
> *The Mexican replied, "Only a little while."*
>
> *The American then asked why he didn't stay out longer and catch more fish? The Mexican said he had*

enough to support his family's immediate needs. The American then asked, "But what do you do with the rest of your time?"

The Mexican fisherman said, "I sleep late, fish a little, play with my children, take siesta with my wife, Maria, stroll into the village each evening where I sip wine and play guitar with my amigos. I have a full and busy life."

The American scoffed, "I have a Harvard MBA and can help you. You should spend more time fishing, and with the proceeds buy a bigger boat, and with the proceeds from the bigger boat buy several boats. Eventually, you could have a fleet of fishing boats. Instead of selling your catch to a middleman, you could sell directly to the processor, eventually opening your own cannery. You would control the product, processing, and distribution. You would need to leave this small coastal fishing village and move to Mexico City, then L.A., and eventually New York, where you would run your expanding enterprise."

The Mexican fisherman asked, "But how long will this take?"

To which the American replied, "Fifteen to 20 years."

"But what then?"

The American laughed and said, "That's the best part. When the time is right, you would announce an IPO and sell your company stock to the public and become very rich. You would make millions."

"Millions?" asked the fisherman, "Then what?"

The American said, "Then you would retire. Move to a small coastal fishing village where you would sleep late, fish a little, play with your kids, take siesta with

*your wife, stroll to the village in the evening, sip wine,
and play your guitar with your amigos!"*

(Author Unknown)[17]

This parable perfectly illustrates the last dimension in
this chapter: Being versus Doing. As discussed throughout this book, the core of American culture is built upon
individualism, personal freedom, and upward mobility.

The American Dream is about becoming whoever you
want. Americans are doers. But not all cultures share
this focus on *doing*. Some focus on *being*.

The Harvard MBA in the story is all about doing.
The Mexican fisherman is focused on being.

Whether you're working with MBAs or fishermen, a core
principle of successful selling (and hey—we're all selling
something) is the ability to quit thinking about what *you*
want and focus on how you can help your prospects get
what *they* want. The Being versus Doing dimension will
help you observe behavior, rethink your own perception,
and answer the question, "What *do* they really want?"

The *Usual Suspects* moment

One of the most vivid *aha* moments I've ever witnessed
happened in New Jersey in April of 2015. I was leading a
cultural-intelligence workshop with a group of
construction-supply sales representatives and had just
finished telling the story of the Jimmy John's sign when a
loud chuckle erupted from the back of the room.

I quickly asked for this gentleman's thoughts.

"Oh, man . . ." the sales rep groaned. "I'm having a *Usual
Suspects* moment right now. Remember at the end of that
movie, when all the pieces of the story come together for
the detective? It becomes so obvious to him, and he drops
his coffee mug on the floor?"

Apparently only half the group knew the movie, but I encouraged him to continue anyway, curious where this was leading.

"Well, I've got this Hispanic customer, and he runs a great business. He has ten employees and they are all relatives. His customers love him and he's a solid, midsize account for me. For the last three years, I've made it one of my goals to help him grow his business—so I can grow mine."

This guy was rolling now.
He stood up.

"Every year, I schedule a formal lunch with him and lay out my plans to help him double his business—connect him with the companies I know that are actively looking for the very services he provides. I talk about how we can help him grow, the credit we can provide, the training we can deliver to his new employees."

He started shaking his head again slowly, replaying those meetings in his mind.

"How does the owner react?" I asked.

"He's always very respectful. He listens closely but never asks any questions. He nods his head a lot and thanks me for all the effort I put in. But then he never does anything with it. Never calls the prospects I give him. Never says anything to me about growing his business, until I set up another meeting the following year.

"When I heard that Jimmy John's story, it just occurred to me . . . maybe he doesn't *want* to grow his business. His company is a well-oiled machine. All his employees are trusted family members. They make good money. Maybe he's happy where he is right now."

Being cultures

Here are a few specific characteristics of a *being* culture. As the eighth and final cultural dimension, you'll see elements of other dimensions affecting being cultures.

BEING v. DOING

HISPANIC
CULTURES

U.S.A.
CULTURE

Being
Work to live

Doing
Live to work

Source: Dr. David Livermore, Leading with Cultural Intelligence

Status shall be given and respected

The fifth cultural dimension in this chapter, Trust, talked about baseline levels of trust. Hispanic cultures have a lower baseline level of trust for outsiders, individuals outside of their in-group.

Status, and the respect that comes with it, however, is given.

This correlates with Hispanic cultures' high Power Distance Index score—a high degree of comfort with the level of inequality among those at the bottom and top of the social stratus.

Harmony shall be maintained

The first cultural dimension, Individualism versus Collectivism, posed the question "Who am I?"

Hispanic cultures are collectivist cultures, which places an emphasis on group harmony. Personal opinions are generally secondary to the opinion of the group. The group dynamic dictates confrontation and disagreement taboo, lest the group descends into chaos.

Faces shall be saved

Being cultures overlap significantly with the relationship-based paradigm (recall the cultural approaches laid out by Erin Meyer, author of *The Culture Map*: relationship-based trust versus task-based trust). *Being* cultures are all about being with other people. The emphasis is on building and maintaining relationships. In Hispanic cultures, causing people to lose face is one of the fastest ways to sever a relationship—or trust.

Time shall *not* be of the essence

While music artist Phil Collins is not Hispanic, his "You Can't Hurry Love" lyrics are an instruction manual for those selling to Hispanics (like I said, everyone is selling something) and the *being* cultural mind-set:

> *You can't hurry love.*
> *No, you just have to wait.*
> *You gotta trust, give it time.*
> *No matter how long it takes.*

Forget your sales funnel and your linear AIDA (**A**wareness, **I**nterest, **D**esire, **A**ction) sales process. In business settings, relationships and trust will take as much time as needed.

Agreement versus understanding

After the sales rep shared his aha moment with the group, realizing his customer didn't want to grow his business, I tried to transition back to my presentation, but was cut off.

"Now let me be clear," the sales rep continued, "a business owner not wanting to grow his business still baffles me, but I understand his perspective a lot more now."

Like all the cultural dimensions discussed in this book, you don't have to agree with them. You just have to try to understand them.

Some cultures identify with the Harvard MBA.
Some identify with the Mexican fisherman.

Neither one is better than the other.

They are simply two different ways to view the world, to live a life. The more you learn about and understand those differences, the better you'll be able to relate to your workers and foster a stronger, more supportive work force.

Now that you have learned several fundamental facts about the Hispanic demographic (Chapter 1); examined historical, geographical, political, and culinary facets of the top five Hispanic countries of origin (Chapter 2); and, most recently, focused on eight cultural elements that affect how people think and act (Chapter 3), it is now time to transition toward language fundamentals.

While Part I focused on the culture (what you do), in Part II you will uncover the most efficient, relevant, and enjoyable ways to expand your Spanish-speaking skills.

Vámonos.
Let's go.

4

Secret of the Spanish Twins

GOOD TO *EXCELENTE* FRAMEWORK™

AWARENESS OF CULTURE

| RECOGNIZE + ACCEPT LA REALIDAD | UNDERSTAND THE ORIGINS | DISTINGUISH AMONG THE DIMENSIONS |

AWARENESS OF LANGUAGE

| SECRET OF THE SPANISH TWINS | EMBRACE THE EQUATION | FORWARD WITH (MICRO) FLUENCY |

Speaking Spanish supports no agenda other than ensuring your future and getting your order right at the taquería. Spanish is no longer a subject juniors sleep through in high school; it's the fourth most spoken language in the world . . . So better practice Spanish as mucho as possible to ensure your future.

—Gustavo Arrellano,
 ¡Ask a Mexican!

SECRET OF THE SPANISH TWINS

SEÑORITA GODÍNEZ MENTIONED THE CONCEPT so casually,
I thought I had misunderstood.

"Er, *un momentito, por favor. Puede*— Er, um, can you . . .
repeat-o . . . that?" I muttered, excitedly.

It was the second week of my freshman-year high school
Spanish class. I remember it all like it was just *ayer*
("yesterday") . . . Our class was located in the basement of
my 75-year-old school. The quarter-inch wood paneling
that lined the walls was not sufficient to improve the look
of the place or to repel the pungent odor of mildew, which
bathed you upon entry.

Educational scenery aside, I loved this class. Growing up
in Elgin, Illinois, in the northwest suburbs of Chicago, I
found the prospect of learning Spanish to be immensely
practical—Elgin is a diverse city of about 110,000 people,
nearly 45 percent of whom are Hispanic.

And now, apparently, there was a simple—and faster—
way to learn it.

"*Por supuesto, Igor*. You mean, *cognates*?" Señorita
Godínez confirmed.

Por supuesto means "of course."
Igor was my Spanish name.[1]

"*Sí. Puede* . . . Can you . . . explain that again?"

"*Por supuesto*. Cognates are words from different
languages that come from the same linguistic family.
They are identical in meaning and similar in spelling and
pronunciation. For example, you asked me to *explain* that
again."

She enunciated the word "explain."

With her Spanish accent, it had three syllables:
(ayks-**PLAH**-een).

"*Explain* is an example of a cognate," Godínez revealed,
scribbling both words on the chalkboard. "In Spanish, it is
explicar. You can see both words share the same
beginning letters, E-X-P-L."

Explain = *Explicar*

"*Explain* and *explicar* are relatives, or cognates. Cognates
are an easy way to learn words of another language—
because you already know the basic form of the word, or
cognate, in your own language. Does this make sense,
Señor Igor?"

Whoa, I thought.
This is huge.

"*Uh, sí. Por supuesto*," I parroted. "How many cognates
are there, uh, *en español*?" I asked.

"*Ay, Dios mío*," *la profesora* said, glancing at the yellow-
stained gypsum ceiling panels. "Thousands."

My jaw dropped.
This was a revelation.
This . . . was . . . *amazing!*

Instead of learning an entire language from scratch, there
were thousands of words that we, as fluent English
speakers, already knew. All we had to do was learn how
to pronounce them!

I glanced around the room, curious to see if any of my
classmates had understood as I had the enormous impact
this could have on our learning potential.

Blank stares. Guess I was the only emerging Spanish
nerd here.

"Is there a class that focuses entirely on these cognates?" I asked.

Boredom-strained laughter trickled out from the class. Señorita Godínez chuckled too.

I was totally serious.

"No, Igor. *Los cognatos* are only one small part of learning a language," she said kindly. "Now, let's start memorizing the conjugation tables for the irregular verb *ir*."

Wait a minute, I thought, *conjugation tables?!*

Back in 1992, the term "WTF" hadn't yet come into fashion, but that was my exact sentiment. I was dumbfounded. Apparently, there were thousands of Spanish words out there that were identical or nearly the same in spelling and meaning to their English counterparts. This was a very encouraging discovery and a promising first step toward my goal of building a vocabulary and speaking the language. And yet *la profesora* simply mentions a few examples and transitions into the annoying world of *grammar*?

This was like Indiana Jones finding the Sankara stones in *Temple of Doom* and telling Short Round, "Nah, kid. Forget it. Leave 'em be. It's not our job to rid the world of child slavery and human sacrifice."

My classmates dozed off. Teaching rules of grammar is the linguistic equivalent of a tryptophan-induced Thanksgiving-dinner coma. It's an exercise in the initiation of sleep.

But I wasn't tired. I was onto something.

I took out my Spanish dictionary and a pen. After flipping through just a few pages, I circled nearly 20 cognates.

I'd done it. I'd discovered (with a little help) the secret of the Spanish Twins.

The formation of the Spanish Twin canon

There are seven shades of Spanish Twins. We'll quickly review each twin category and provide you with some examples that should be relevant for you on the job. And although there are indeed thousands of Spanish Twins, as Señorita Godínez pointed out, I'm not going to belabor the point by going over all of them.

Remember the MED: minimum effective dose. The goal of this book is to get you up to speed on the basics of Hispanic culture and the Spanish language. If this chapter particularly intrigues you, you can learn a whole lot more in my book *Spanish Twins: Start Speaking Spanish on the Construction Site with Words You Already Know.*

1. Identical Spanish Twins

This first shade of Spanish Twins is pretty straightforward. With a few slight exceptions, the following table of words are identical in spelling and meaning in both English and Spanish. Master the pronunciation and you're all set. I consider these the Holy Grail of vocabulary acquisition.

ajustable	digital	imposible	natural
área	doctor	laser	plan
auto	durable	material	posible
base	error	memorable	principal
cable	final	mental	regular
capital	horizontal	metal	vertical
color	hospital	motor	visór

2. Irish Spanish Twins

For Irish Spanish Twins, we take Spanish words that are already mostly identical to their English counterparts and simply add an *o*.

Think of some common Irish last names.

O'Reilly. O'Shea. Oh, Danny Boy.

¿Comprende?

The only difference here is that we're adding the *o* at the *end* of the word, not the beginning.

This might already sound familiar to you. Have you ever been around a friend who pretended to speak Spanish by doing this? "Hey-o, can-o I-o order-o another-o beer-o, amigo-o?"

Right. First of all, don't ever do this. It's not actually that funny. Secondly, it's also offensive, even if only mildly so because Anglos do it with such frequency.

That being said . . . there's a lot of truth to your friend's "comedic" butchering of the Spanish language. What he's doing is just trying to make use of some of the Irish Spanish Twins out there—and there are a ton of them.

aditivo	cono	incorrecto	proceso
automático	correcto	minuto	producto
cemento	costo	mucho	rápido
círculo	efecto	momento	sófito
concreto	experto	perfecto	tubo
completo	fantástico	plástico	verbo

3. Fonzie Spanish Twins

Fonzie Spanish Twins are named after none other than Arthur Herbert Fonzarelli, aka "The Fonz," from the *Happy Days* sitcom, from the '70s and '80s. His signature, guttural catch phrase was, "AAAAAAEEEEEE!" an adaptive utterance of approval that he used often. It was applicable in any number of situations, such as when a cute girl gave him a back massage or when his tuna melt arrived promptly after arriving at Arnold's Restaurant.

Fonzie Spanish Twins are equally flexible. These Spanish Twins simply add an *a* or an *e* to the end of the (mostly) English word.

batería	jamba	rampa	cliente
curva	línea	sistema	grande
demanda	nota	yarda	importante
emergencia	persona	accidente	presidente
forma	problema	agente	residente
gasolina	programa	aire	tripode

4. Infinity verbs

All verbs in Spanish end in one of three endings: *-ar*, *-er*, and *-ir*. To pronounce them, the emphasis is always on the last syllable. To borrow a couple Irish Spanish Twins, these two rules are *sólido* ("solid") and ones you can take to the *banco* ("bank").

Grammatically speaking, these verbs are called *infinitives*. Infinitives are actually pretty straightforward: it's just the word "to" followed by a verb. But because the term itself isn't very intuitive, it tends to obscure more than it reveals.

That's why I like to call them *Infinity* verbs. The term itself is a bit more recognizable—plus it describes one of the useful attributes of these words. Infinity verbs need no conjugation, meaning, they don't have different endings depending on who is speaking (for example, I, you, he, she, it). We can simply add them after another verb such as *Necesitas* (nay-say-**SEE**-tahs), which means "You need," and then use it forever and ever . . . until infinity.

For example, *Necesitas instalar, Necesitas reparar, Necesitas mover,* etc. Ignore the *-ar, -er,* and *-ir* endings in the terms below and you'll see plenty of action verbs you can use. Then practice saying *Necesitas.* Use it in front of the verb, and you will be effectively communicating what action *needs to be done.*

admitir	excavar	permitir	resolver
ajustar	formar	practicar	responder
completar	instalar	preferir	transportar
continuar	mover	preparar	usar
costar	observar	presentar	utilizar
describir	organizar	recomendar	visitar

5. *See-Own* Spanish Twins

English words that end in the *-tion* or *-sion* suffix and make a "shun" sound are overwhelmingly Spanish Twins. Think *installation, inspection, function,* and *erosion.* Say them casually in English and you'll hear the "shun" sound at the end. Got it?

In Spanish, the pronunciation of the cognate suffix, *-ción,* is not as intuitive. When English speakers attempt to guess at the Spanish pronunciation, it often sounds like a linguistic car crash between Italian and German.

"OK, here I go. Ahem. *Inspección* . . .
In-spehk-chee-**OH**-nee? How was that?"

After hearing hundreds of these attempts, I realized it wasn't a learning disability—it was a *teaching* disability. I made one minor change to the pronunciation explanation and language learners picked it up in no time.

The "shun" sound at the end of *inspección*, for example, sounds like two English words smushed together: **SEE + OWN**. When you see a *See-Own* Spanish Twin (and there are hundreds of them for you to guess at), you want to *SEE* it and *OWN* it.

So, let's try again, Señor Language Learner.

"OK, I'm still nervous. Ahem. *Inspección* . . . In-spehk-see-**OWN**. Better?"

Definitely.

To reinforce the fact that SEE + OWN is a single syllable in Spanish—the stressed syllable, in fact—I use **SYOHN** for the phonetic sound. It's not perfect, but once the foundation (*¡fundación!*) of SEE + OWN is in place, SYOHN is easy to identify.

ac**ción**	fertiliza**ción**	instruc**ción**	renova**ción**
aten**ción**	filtra**ción**	intimida**ción**	situa**ción**
condi**ción**	fun**ción**	oca**sión**	solu**ción**
deci**sión**	globaliza**ción**	posi**ción**	trac**ción**
educa**ción**	infiltra**ción**	prohibi**ción**	ventila**ción**
ero**sión**	inspec**ción**	protec**ción**	visualiza**ción**

6. Dad Spanish Twins
A majority of the words that end in *-ity* in English end in *-idad* (or the occasional *-edad*) in Spanish. For example, the Spanish Twin for *electricity* is *electric**idad***.

Similar to *See-Own* Spanish Twins, feel free to guess at the Spanish Twin. When you've summoned the courage to engage Spanish speakers on the job and are mentally fumbling for the Spanish word *job*, remember a synonym like *activity* ends in *-ity* and guess *actividad* with confidence.

PRONUNCIATION PRO TIP

All Dad Spanish Twins stress the last syllable—the *-idad* syllable.

---

activi**dad**	electrici**dad**	necesi**dad**	reali**dad**
adversi**dad**	eterni**dad**	negativi**dad**	superiori**dad**
capaci**dad**	hume**dad**	oportuni**dad**	universi**dad**
cavi**dad**	identi**dad**	posibili**dad**	utili**dad**
densi**dad**	nacionali**dad**	propie**dad**	veloci**dad**

7. *Mente* Spanish Twins

The last group of Spanish Twins we'll review are called *Mente* Spanish Twins. Pronounced (**MAYN**-tay), this is the Spanish equivalent of the English adverb ending *-ly*.

Read the Spanish Twins *en Español* below and simply substitute *–ly* in place of *-mente*.

absoluta**mente**	especial**mente**	incorrecta**mente**	rapida**mente**
accidental**mente**	eventual**mente**	inmediata**mente**	real**mente**
casual**mente**	evidente**mente**	natural**mente**	reciente**mente**
completa**mente**	exacta**mente**	normal**mente**	simple**mente**
correcta**mente**	final**mente**	original**mente**	total**mente**
directa**mente**	horizontal**mente**	perfecta**mente**	vertical**mente**

So what?
Well, the preceding pages just introduced you to 168 new Spanish words, which, with minimal cognitive effort, you can practice saying on your own in Spanish.

Now what?
Good question. Now we will introduce a single word that will allow you to start lining up these Spanish Twins into relevant sentences that you can use immediately.

PUEDE
(**PWAY**-day)
Can you

The *Puede* Payday
The Spanish verb *puede* can help you create relevant sentences in Spanish immediately. It's the Spanish equivalent of the English verb *can you*. In English, we use it to say things like:

- *Can you start this?*
- *Can you finish that?*
- *Can you move this?*
- *Can you repair that?*

We can use *puede* in the same way, and then sequence any number of Spanish Twins right after it.

At Red Angle, we refer to this as "The *Puede* Payday," because once you lock this bad boy down, *payday comes every day*. And it's healthier for you than an actual Payday candy bar, which is chock full of high-fructose corn syrup, nuts, caramel, and nougat.

Let's line 'em up...

To demonstrate how we can start assembling these
Spanish Twin phrases, let's begin with a simple equation:

Puede + Infinity Spanish Twin + Identical Spanish Twin

Remember: Infinity Spanish Twins are verbs that end in
-*ar*, -*er*, or –*ir*, such as *completar*, *responder*, and
describir. And Identical Spanish Twins are just that—
pretty much identical to their English equivalent.

I'll start you off with a few examples.
Then you make three of your own.

¿Puede reparar el error?
Can you repair the error?

¿Puede mover el material?
Can you move the material?

¿Puede instalar el metal?
Can you install the metal?

Not so hard, right?
Now, make three sentences of your own.

¿Puede _____ *el/la* _____?
Can you _____ the _____?

¿Puede _____ *el/la* _____?
Can you _____ the _____?

¿Puede _____ *el/la* _____?
Can you _____ the _____?

Bueno.

Now let's repeat the same exercise with this equation:

Puede + *Infinity Spanish Twin (verb)* + *Irish Spanish Twin*

Remember: Irish Spanish Twins are, essentially, Identical Spanish Twins with an *o* added at the end of the word.

¿Puede completar el sófito?
Can you complete the soffit?

¿Puede continuar el proceso?
Can you continue the process?

¿Puede ajustar el tubo?
Can you adjust the tube?

Now you . . .

¿Puede _____ *el/la* _____?
Can you _____ the _____?

¿Puede _____ *el/la* _____?
Can you _____ the _____?

¿Puede _____ *el/la* _____?
Can you _____ the _____?

¿Puede _____ *el/la* _____?
Can you _____ the _____?

¿Puede _____ *el/la* _____?
Can you _____ the _____?

Putting them all together

Now, let's assemble some sentences with *all* our Spanish Twin options on the table. Feel free to use *de* ("of," "from") and *en* ("in," "on") as connector words to build stronger sentences. These are called "high-frequency words," the most commonly used words in any language. We'll go over these in more detail in Chapter 5.

Puede + Infinity Spanish Twin + Identical Spanish Twin + Mente Spanish Twin

¿Puede instalar el material verticalmente?
Can you install the material vertically?

Puede + Infinity Spanish Twin + Identical Spanish Twin + Fonzie Spanish Twin

¿Puede mover la base de cemento en la rampa?
Can you move the cement base on the ramp?

Puede + Infinity Spanish Twin + Identical Spanish Twin + Dad Spanish Twin

¿Puede completar la inspección de la electricidad?
Can you complete the inspection of the electricity?

Normalmente, puede ajustar la insulación en la cavidad.
Normally, you can adjust the insulation in the cavity.

Now you can assemble your own. Don't worry about perfection—just have fun putting words together that you (now) know.

¿Puede_____?

Can you _____?

¿Puede_____?

Can you _____?

¿Puede_____?

Can you _____?

¿Puede_____?

Can you _____?

In this chapter, you saw firsthand how Spanish Twins can help eliminate much of the pain and frustration that typically welcomes a language learner. Spanish Twins are a key step in the MED (minimum effective dose—but you know that by now). The next thing you have to consider is their accurate pronunciation, a topic we'll simplify next.

5

Embrace the Equation

GOOD TO *EXCELENTE* FRAMEWORK™

AWARENESS OF CULTURE

RECOGNIZE + ACCEPT *LA REALIDAD*	UNDERSTAND THE ORIGINS	DISTINGUISH AMONG THE DIMENSIONS

AWARENESS OF LANGUAGE

SECRET OF THE SPANISH TWINS	EMBRACE THE EQUATION	FORWARD WITH (MICRO) FLUENCY

From the time we're small, we hear this good advice from our parents and teachers: Take it a little bit at a time. *This advice works because it accurately reflects the way our brains learn. Every skill is built out of smaller pieces—what scientists call chunks.*

—Daniel Coyle,
  The Little Book of Talent

EMBRACE THE EQUATION

NOW THAT YOU'VE LEARNED THE SECRET (and power!) of
the Spanish Twins, your perspective on the language
should be evolving a bit. Retaining a few hundred
relevant Spanish words isn't that difficult after all, is it?
Despite what little you may have thought about your
language-acquisition capabilities, perhaps you just
needed a different teaching method to help make things
click.

After coaching thousands of managers and training more
than 100 companies, I've found that the key to learning
anything involves one simple equation: M=REB.

Memorability = Relevance + Entertainment + Brevity

When people think of corporate training, what they
typically imagine is really the *inverse* of M=REB.
Their assumption is that the content will be somewhat
irrelevant, mostly boring, painfully long, and ultimately
forgettable. Learning—and retaining—anything that way
can obviously be challenging.

However, if the content is relevant to the learner,
entertaining (even *mildly* so, as I'll demonstrate), and
brief, the memorability usually takes care of itself.

M=REB is the key to retaining new language. In this
chapter, we'll be putting that equation to work.

There's no such thing as memorization
The second course in my MBA program was a comm-
unications class. It was basically Speech Comm 101 for
adults. Ten weeks of public speaking. Each of our
performances was recorded. And at the end of the term,
we each received a cute, little mini-CD with all of our
performances on it.

Each week, our performances incorporated a different style.

One was a slideshow presentation. One was an extemporaneous presentation, where we had to present new material on the spot without preparation. One was a "bad news" presentation that we pretended to give to a live, angry audience.

And in one particularly memorable presentation, I donned all my snowboarding gear and recited Lewis Carroll's poem "Jabberwocky."[1] (Don't ask.)

"Jabberwocky" is a seven-stanza poem with 167 words, many of which are completely nonsensical, like *frabjous*, *frumious*, *manxome*, and *galumphing*—words that beg to be autocorrected (and were born of an author who happened to be clacking away at his typewriter while high on opioids).

"With all these nonsense words in the poem," my professor had told us, "You'll never be able to *learn* it— you'll just have to memorize it."

The class groaned, and with good reason—there is no such thing as memorization. Seriously.

In his book *Fluent Forever*, author Gabriel Wyner makes an interesting observation. While we've all been directed to memorize something at some point in our lives, how many of us ever recall being taught *how* to memorize it? At best, it seems like mere repetition.[2]

What's the process?

"We can think, we can repeat, we can recall, and we can imagine," Wyner writes, "but we are not built to memorize."

Your brain is, essentially, a filter—and an incredibly effective one at that, given the millions of inputs we hear, see, feel, touch, and taste every day. The human brain is constantly processing information—filtering out the unimportant (*Hey look, the A in the Samsung logo has no crossbar!*) and saving the important (*I think my wife's birthday is tomorrow . . .*).

If your brain let everything through—that is, if everything was deemed to have the same mental value—you'd go insane. It would be total sensory overload.

Wyner explains:

> *"Your brain uses levels of processing to determine which input is important and which should be thrown out. You don't want to be thinking about the number of letters in the word tiger when one is chasing after you, nor do you want to be assaulted by vivid memories of cows when you buy milk."*

But how do you determine if something is worth remembering?

There are four levels of mental processing we use to separate the cognitive wheat from the chaff, as it were: structure, sound, concept, and personal connection.

In this next section, we will examine each level of processing and will do so with the help of one of the most fundamental items found on the construction jobsite: the hardhat.

The four levels of (mental) word processing

1. Structure

At the structural level of processing, you're simply examining the word—that's all at this stage. So let's start with ours: *el casco*, or "hardhat." Examine the word and see what you notice. For example, you likely recognize that *el* is a short word with only two letters. *Casco*, of course, is longer with five letters. Your brain then quickly dances around the two *C*s as it considers the next level of processing.

2. Sound

If you have ever taken a foreign-language class before, this part should feel familiar. If we were in a language class now, the instructor would encourage everyone to say *el casco* in unison.

el casco :: (ayl **KAHS**-koh) :: hardhat

Your brain processes the phonetics of the term (ayl **KAHS**-koh) and recognizes that both *C*s in *casco* are hard *C*s. They sound like *K*s.

You notice the *A* in *casco* sounds like saying "AHHH," the international sound of tongue depressors. You repeat it a few more times.

el casco :: (ayl **KAHS**-koh) :: hardhat

The instructor tells you Spanish is a phonetic language. Words sound the same all the time.

The instructor gives you an example. Consider the different ways we pronounce the letter *A* depending on the English word. Say the following words to yourself to see what I mean.

apple (ah)
almond (au)
able (ay)
father (ah, but different than *apple*, right?)
about (uh)
private (ih)

All over the place, right?

Luckily, you already know that Spanish is a phonetic language. You can trust Spanish sounds. So you practice your new Spanish word one more time.

el casco :: (ayl **KAHS**-koh) :: hardhat

3. Concept
Given your knowledge of the construction profession, you are already well aware of what a hardhat is. Now we just need a way to bridge the gap between what you already know and something you're trying to learn: *el casco*. To do that, we will connect the unfamiliar word to a familiar concept—or what Wyner describes as a "concrete, multisensory experience."

Have you ever shopped at Costco?

You know, the giant warehouse retailer where you can buy 400 pounds of Purina Puppy Chow, a set of snow tires, two-gallon containers of shampoo, a tankful of live lobsters, and a new pair of pleated dad khakis—all under the same ginormous roof?

It's wonderful.

Well, Costco and *casco* are pronounced nearly the same way. Go easy on the *T* sound in Costco and you arrive at *casco*.

What we're doing here is connecting a concept you already know (the store Costco) with a new word you're trying to remember, *el casco*. To increase the memorability factor here, I'll include the following image.

See what I did there? Notice the pair of *cascos* sitting on top the of the Costco logo.

Wyner notes that "image-recall studies have repeatedly demonstrated that our visual memory is phenomenal . . . we only need to learn how to take advantage of it."

This makes intuitive sense.

Visit a construction site and you'll see evidence everywhere of our predilection for visuals. We start any project with literal drawings (hopefully) and then we draw on top of them (redlines). We draw on concrete floors, on studs and drywall, and most frequently on the inside walls of the Port-A-Potties.

4. Personal connection
"You will remember a concept with a personal connection 50 percent more easily than a concept without one," Wyner notes.

So let's do that. One Saturday each month, let's say, your significant other informs you it's time to head to Costco. You're running low on toilet paper and you need a keg of extra virgin olive oil. As you exit the car, your partner says, "Honey—don't forget your *casco*. You have to wear your *casco* whenever we shop at Costco."

Remembering that Costco stacks their pallets of Cocoa Puffs and Fruity Pebbles 100 feet high, you grab your *casco* and put it on. *Yep*, you think, *gotta wear my casco in Costco!*

Creating this personal connection—linking an experience you've had multiple times with a new word—is effective because of how your brain works. The neurons in your brain are firing constantly, processing input from all over the place. The sensory recall of visiting Costco is processed vividly in your brain: The faint sounds of forklifts moving merchandise. The smell of unfettered commerce. The excitement of cost savings that accompanies the purchase of four giant boxes of Froot Loops cereal taped together. It all sticks.

And, of course, there's the slight embarrassment you feel walking into Costco wearing your *casco*. Until you imagine everyone shopping at Costco is wearing a *casco* as well—just to help make the image stick in your mind a little more.

These four levels of mental word processing might seem like a lot to absorb, but I guarantee you it clicks quickly. Remember the "B" in M=REB: *Brevity*. This extends to my Red Angle workshops as well. During those, I'll introduce the word *el casco* and then run through these four levels in less than a minute.

First, I'll show the word on screen and define it, then I'll say it aloud a few times, noting how *casco* has only five letters whereas "hardhat" has seven. Then I'll mention the "AHH" sound and ask the group to say it aloud. Then I'll call on a few individuals to say it so everyone can hear their pronunciation.

Next, I'll flash an aerial view of Costco, make a few jokes about the magic of the place, and then show the image from earlier.

And the whole time I'm doing all this, the various connections are being made on all four levels of processing.

Let's run through them quickly one more time.

Structure: We get acquainted with the word, looking at the letter count.

el casco :: (ayl **KAHS**-koh) :: hardhat

Sound: We say the word aloud, evaluate its phonetics, and practice it.

Concept: We connect *casco* the word to Costco the place.

Personal connection: We incorporate important people in your life and link the word to a routine shopping experience at Costco. Then we help you imagine actually donning your *casco* as you stroll into Costco, prepared to debit card your way to happiness.

CASCO FURY... AND RETENTION

Recently, I was yelled at by an old construction-site safety guy. You know the type. In his mid-60s. Born on the jobsite during a November concrete pour. Has forgotten more about construction than I'll ever learn. Is happiest when he is unhappy.

Yeah, you know the type.

"Hey, Red!" he yelled, not a few feet behind me, referring to my ginger-colored hair. The aggressive tone was out of place, as we were at an industry conference, having a beer at the end of a long day. I wheeled around, concerned.

"I've been meaning to talk to you about your Spanish stuff," he declared. How can someone be so angry with a Coors Light in his hand, I thought.

"I saw you speak three years ago. And now I think of you just about every week—and I'm not happy about it."

"I'm sorry to hear that. Sounds terrible," I admitted.

"There's a Costco a mile from my house. Every time I drive past it or my wife drags me along to shop there, I think of you . . . And your stupid red hardhat. Or rather, your stupid red *casco*."

"Looks like old dogs can learn new tricks," I quipped, fighting fire with fire. "You're welcome." He smiled.

Remember, there is no such thing as memorization. You can, however, remember just about anything when you process new words with deeper thought using structure, sound, concept, and personal connection.

Lucky for you, new Spanish terms like *casco* are relevant and useful. As for my "Jabberwocky" recitation skills?

Not so much.

Checking the *casco* math. . .
Let's check the *casco* example using the M=REB equation.

Relevant: Yes. Hardhats are relevant on construction sites.

Entertaining: Admittedly, this was a bit shy of, say, a Louis C.K. standup act, but the story here should have (hopefully) captured your attention.

Brief: As I mentioned, in-person I can bang out this *casco* story in about 60 seconds. Reading it took a little longer, but not much.

Memorability: Whether you like it or not, the next time you drive by a Costco or visit one, I'll bet you two push-ups you remember the Spanish word for "hardhat" (which, of course, is *casco*).

Sounding Spanish
In this section, I've distilled the basics of Spanish pronunciation down to four elements: two places, one culinary godsend, and Vince Vaughn.

The two places are Las Vegas, Nevada, and La Jolla, California. The food item is the almighty burrito. And Vince Vaughn is, well, Vince Vaughn.

That's it.

Now let's unpack these for you so that they make sense, stick in your head, and ultimately help your Spanish pronunciation sound more *excelente*.

1. The Las Vegas Rule of Pronunciation
No one mispronounces Las Vegas. The reason for this—aside from the global renown of the Sin City—is largely because Spanish is a phonetic language, meaning the

letters always sound the same. They don't change. In Spanish, the *A* makes an "AHH" sound.

"AHHHH" yes. Laaas Vegas.

As noted in the *casco* discussion earlier, the English letter *A* can sound like a lot of different things: apple, agent, arrange . . . you get the idea. In Spanish, however, it stays put.

taco :: (**TAH**-koh)
salsa :: (**SAHL**-sah)
adios :: (**AH**-dee-ohs)

In the word *Vegas*, the *E* makes an "AY" sound. That's always consistent in Spanish.

siesta :: (see-**AY**-stah)
cerveza :: (sayr-**BAY**-sah)
Mesa (Arizona) :: (**MAY**-sah)

2. The La Jolla Rule of Pronunciation
La Jolla, the beautiful seaside town in San Diego, California, is a helpful example for learning two Spanish pronunciation rules that aren't immediately intuitive. So let's make sure we're all saying "La Jolla" correctly, because it definitely isn't pronounced how you might think it would be in English.

La Jolla :: (lah **HOY**-yah)

There are a couple things going on here with "Jolla" that might be unfamiliar to you.

First off, the *J*s in "Jolla" are pronounced like *H*s.

In case that was confusing, let me say it again: In Spanish, *J*s are pronounced like *H*s: think of the names José (ho-**SAY**) or Julio (**HOOH**-lee-oh) or Jesus (**HAY**-zeus).

PRONUNCIATION PRO TIP

Relevant to note here is that *H*s in Spanish are always silent. Here are a few examples:

Hola (**OH**-lah) hello
Hombre (**OHM**-bray) man
Hoy (**OY**) today
Hacer (ah-**SAYR**) to do
Hogar (oh-**GAHR**) home

Second, you'll note that La Jolla includes a pair of *L*s. The double "L" sound in Spanish sounds like a *Y* in English.

For example, think about the Texas city of Amarillo, which has the same double-*L* sound in La Jolla.

Amarillo :: (ah-mah-**REE**-yoh)

Amarillo means "yellow" in Spanish. So to help you remember how to pronounce the double *L*s in *Amarillo*, just think of the *Y* in yellow. (Just don't pronounce the double *L*s in yellow as a *Y* as well or people might look at you funny . . .)

3. The Burrito Rule of Pronunciation

Burrito :: (booh-**REE**-toh)

Saying burrito, we notice the *U* makes an "OOH" sound. It's the same "OOH" sound we hear in "food" or Cancún.

Cancún :: (kahn-**KOON**)
Burrito :: (booh-**REE**-toh)

All *U*s make this sound in Spanish.

Next, we focus on the *I* in *burrito*. It sounds like the English letter *E*, right?

To practice your phonetics, think of the menu at Taco Bell:

gordita :: (gohr-**DEE**-tah)
cantina :: (kahn-**TEE**-nah)
quesadilla :: (kay-sah-**DEE**-yah)
enchirito :: (ayn-chee-**REE**-toh)

See how the *I* makes an *E* sound?

Bueno.

4. The Bince Baughn Rule of Pronunciation

The reason I've butchered world-renowned thespian Vince Vaughn's name here is to demonstrate how all *V*s in Spanish sound like *B*s. I know that might sound odd to an English speaker's ear, so I'll say it again: in Spanish, all *V*s sound like *B*s.

Yes . . . Bince Baughn.

How about Vincent Van Gogh?
Right. Bincent Ban Gogh.

How about Vincent Vega from the movie Pulp Fiction?
Yep. Bincent Bega.

How about Victoria Beckham, the former Spice Girl and wife of pretty-boy soccer legend David Beckham?
Bictoria Beckham.

OK, I think you get the idea.

Quick recap:

The Las Vegas Rule of Pronunciation tells us an *A* in Spanish makes an "AH" sound, and an *E* sounds like "AY."

The La Jolla Rule of Pronunciation tells us a *J* in Spanish makes an "H" sound, and a double *L* makes a "Y" sound.

Quick side note: the Las Vegas and La Jolla rules of pronunciation can be applied to all other Spanish words.

The Burrito Rule or Pronunciation tells us the *U* in Spanish sounds like the *U* in Cancún (the "OOH" sound), and the *I* in Spanish makes an "E" sound.

And lastly, the Bince Baughn Rule of Pronunciation tells us all *V*s in Spanish sound like the English letter *B*.

Remember these four rules of pronunciation to help you learn the lingo—and sound less like a gringo.

Leveraging the Spanish *vocabulario* around you
You can also expand your Spanish vocabulary simply by looking a little more closely at the world around you. In the pages to follow, there are a few examples of how to do just that.

Buckle up.

1. LOOK AT A MAP

Just by looking at a map—and adding a dash of curiosity—you can help improve your vocabulary.

Cities with Spanish names dot the globe. (Think back to your *Where in the World is Carmen Sandiego?* days . . .) Here are some of my favorites.

TIERRA DEL FUEGO, CHILE
Tierra del Fuego :: (**TYAY**-rrah dayl **FWAY**-goh) :: Land of Fire

There cannot be *that* much fire, given its close proximity to Antarctica at the southern tip of South America.

TORNILLO, TEXAS
tornillo :: (tohr-**NEE**-yoh) :: screw

Remember the La Jolla Rule of Pronunciation with this one—then create your own punchline.

THE STATE OF NEVADA
nevada :: (nay-**BAH**-dah) :: snowfall

When deciding on the state name, apparently the naming delegation visited Lake Tahoe in January. Be sure to channel your inner Bince Baughn when pronouncing this one.

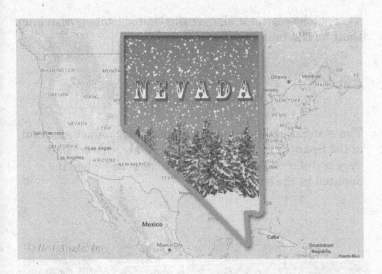

MATANZAS, CUBA
matanzas :: (mah-**TAHN**-sahs) :: killings

Finally, some Cuban truth in advertising!

CERRO GORDO, ILLINOIS
Cerro Gordo :: (**SAY**-rroh **GOHR**-doh) :: Fat Hill

Living in a town with the name Fat Hill has to provide some motivation to exercise.

2. GO CAR SHOPPING

When naming cars, the first stop for many automakers is often a Spanish dictionary. For some, it shouldn't be . . .

KIA RÍO
río :: (**REE**-oh) :: river

This one has Latinos all over the United States scratching their heads. Is it a boat or a car?

CHEVY NOVA
nova :: (noh-**BAH**) :: no go, not going

The standard bearer when it comes to car names ignorant of the Spanish language. Unsurprisingly, this was not very popular in Spanish-speaking countries when it debuted in the early 1960s.

ISUZU HOMBRE
hombre :: (**OHM**-bray) :: man

It's like Isuzu isn't even trying. If you're gonna rip off the Spanish language, get creative! It cannot get any worse than this.

ISUZU AMIGO
amigo :: (ah-**MEE**-goh) :: friend

Nevermind. I spoke too soon—it can get worse. Isuzu Enemigo—"enemy"—would have been a better choice than Amigo.

EL CAMINO
camino :: (kah-**MEE**-noh) :: road, path, route, way

Is it a car? Is it a pickup? Hey now! It's both! And to further reinforce the peculiarity of this vehicle, we'll the name the car . . . The Road. Brilliant!

HONDA DEL SOL
del sol :: (dayl **SOHL**) :: of the sun

Well, if beers can come from the sun, why can't cars? (see *Cerveza Sol* in the next *sección*)

GMC SIERRA
sierra :: (see-**YAY**-rrah) :: saw

Aha. So, that's why so many carpenters drive these! Remember the Las Vegas Rule of Pronunciation with this one.

PORSCHE CARRERA
carrera :: (kah-**RRAY**-rah) :: race, dash

OK, now *this* makes sense. It's rather literal when translated. Isuzu: take note, please.

HYUNDAI TIBURON
tiburón :: (tee-booh-**ROHN**) :: shark

Driving a Tiburon in Matanzas ("Killings"), Cuba, may be too ironic of a vehicle selection for some.

NISSAN MURANO
marrano :: (mah-**RRAH**-noh) :: pig, disgusting

The key to good marketing is identifying a name that's memorable. This . . . is memorable.

3. HAVE A DRINK

This part is just like college—a formal request to mix education and booze.

MODELO ESPECIAL
model :: (moh-**DAY**-loh) :: model
especial :: (ay-spay-see-**AHL**) :: special

Oh yes, this model is special indeed.

CORONA
corona :: (koh-**ROH**-nah) :: crown

If Budweiser is the King (*el rey*) of Beers, then why does Corona have the crown?

TEQUILA AVIÓN
avión :: (ah-bee-**OHN**) :: airplane

Leslie Nielson's and Kareem's favorite tequila, for sure. But remember: Friends don't let friends fly *borracho*.

TEQUILA PATRÓN
patrón :: (pah-**TROHN**) :: boss

This stuff is boss.

CERVEZA SOL
sol :: (**SOHL**) :: sun

Mmmm, warm beer . . .
Wait. No.

4. WATCH ESPN

Athletes all over ESPN are representing the Spanish language. It's only natural that sportscaster Dan Patrick popularized the saying *en fuego* ("on fire").

JOSÉ MESA :: JOSEPH TABLE
mesa :: (**MAY**-sah) :: table

As a dominant closer, Mesa set the table for a win.

IKEA
Joseph Table
$29.00

TONY ARMAS :: TONY WEAPONS
armas :: (**AHR**-mahs) :: weapons, arms

Welcome to the gun show, ladies! It was always NRA night at the ballpark when this Boston Red Sox legend rolled into town . . .

PEDRO GUERRERO :: PETER WARRIOR
guerrero :: (gay-**RRAY**-roh) :: warrior

Fantastic name for anybody!

LAVAR ARRINGTON :: "TO WASH" ARRINGTON
lavar :: (lah-**BAHR**) :: to wash, launder

The second overall pick in the 2000 NFL draft had a solid, albeit somewhat brief, career. After seven seasons, he was all washed up.

Would you like queso with that?
Admittedly, some of the previous examples were a bit, um, cheesy. However, I have consistently found that teaching this way improves retention and maintains interest far better than repetition alone.

The examples above are an extension of the M=REB equation:

Memorability = Relevance + Entertainment + Brevity

From *casco* ("hardhat") to the GMC Sierra ("saw") to José Mesa ("table") to Tornillo ("screw"), Texas, you can see the value in the M=REB equation.

If the content is relevant, entertaining, and brief, the memorability will take care of itself. M=REB is the equation to retaining new-language skills.

When I think of the M=REB equation, I'm reminded of the immortal words of Dean Vernon Wormer, head of the fictional Faber College in the classic 1978 film *Animal House*. While offering advice to one of the poorer-performing students, he says, "Fat, drunk, and stupid is no way to go through life, son."

True.

There's a learning corollary to Dean Wormer's incisive wisdom: irrelevant, boring, and long-winded is no way to learn anything new.

6

Forward with (micro) Fluency

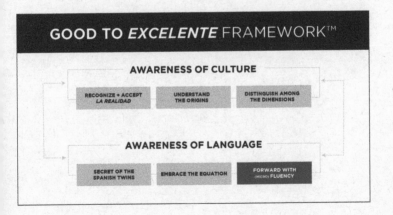

GOOD TO *EXCELENTE* FRAMEWORK™

AWARENESS OF CULTURE

| RECOGNIZE + ACCEPT *LA REALIDAD* | UNDERSTAND THE ORIGINS | DISTINGUISH AMONG THE DIMENSIONS |

AWARENESS OF LANGUAGE

| SECRET OF THE SPANISH TWINS | EMBRACE THE EQUATION | FORWARD WITH (MICRO) FLUENCY |

The greatest enemy of learning a language, especially as an adult, is a person's inhibitions . . . One way to get started is to remember that however silly you might sound using your incorrect Spanish, you'll sound a lot worse trying to speak English to someone who speaks none.

—Joseph J. Keenan,
   Breaking Out of Beginner's Spanish

FORWARD WITH (MICRO) FLUENCY

WHILE WORKING FROM MY STARBUCKS OFFICE ONE MORNING, I noticed two Latino twentysomethings sitting across from me. Their language choices caught my attention.

They were jumping back and forth constantly between English and Spanish. They'd use English to discuss the details of a school project, and then one would switch to Spanish to make fun of the other guy's jeans.

They alternated languages rapidly—even midsentence. An average sentence would look something like this:

ENGLISH NOUN + ENGLISH ADJECTIVE + SPANISH VERB + ENGLISH SLANG + SPANISH SWEAR WORD.

It was interesting to listen in on.

There's a term for what these young men were doing. It's called code-switching. Code-switching is when two or more people speak multiple shared languages and intermix them on the fly.

But what about when two people who don't speak *each other's* language try and intermix them on the fly? What's *that* called?

Confusion and rework, usually.

But not always.

I know several construction managers who are bilingual in very specific situations. They know a handful of words and phrases—maybe 100 to 150—that are applied with confidence but only in certain situations.

They have reached a level of micro-fluency: the achievement of basic conversational and problem-solving skills within a specific domain.

> ## MICRO-FLUENCY
> Achieving basic conversational skills within a specific domain.

For example, I know a landscape manager who is micro-fluent. He has mastered what he calls "Landscape Spanish." If it's related to his job managing his crews, he knows how to say it in Spanish. Things like the following:

- retaining walls
- sod
- shrubbery
- hoses
- watering
- jokes about angry customers with dead sod
- maintenance equipment
- mulch
- swear words

He is micro-fluent in this arena.

Make a joke in Spanish about the Chicago Cubs, however, and he'll look at you with a straight face and say, "No, dude. I only speak Landscape Spanish."

I know an angry, old hunchbacked roofer named Donny. Donny is micro-fluent in roofing.

He manages ten roofing crews. They all speak Spanish, so he became micro-fluent in all things Roofing Spanish:

- architectural shingles
- ice and water shields
- slate

- ladders
- lanyards
- scaffolding
- ridge vents
- weather conditions

If it affects his roofers, he knows how to say it in Spanish. But ask him in Spanish if he's ever been to Mexico, and he'll deadpan to you (as he did to me once), "Speak English, Red. I don't speak Spanish."

Donny is micro-fluent in the roofing arts. Which, of course, is a valuable skill to him, his men, and his company, because being able to communicate clearly and effectively with his team is paramount.

Think about your job. Is there one area where the language barrier causes more pain than it does in others?

Maybe it's paint and drywall? If so, become micro-fluent in paint and drywall. One hundred specific terms relating to paint and drywall will take you a long way toward improving your leadership skills and minimizing your teams' rework.

But how do you achieve the level of micro-fluency needed to make the work on you job run more smoothly? You only need one phrase: *¿Cómo se dice?*

¿CÓMO SE DICE?
(**KOH**-moh say **DEE**-say)
How do you say?

When used as a scripted loop—which we'll cover in the next section—*¿Cómo se dice?* offers the most efficient path toward micro-fluency.

The ¿Cómo se dice? scripted loop

There are four simple steps to leveraging ¿Cómo se dice?
on the job today:

1. Locate a Spanish speaker.
2. Open your mouth.
3. Say "¿Cómo se dice?"
4. Point at something.

That's it.

I recommend establishing a daily ¿Cómo se dice? quota.
Twice each day—once in the morning and once in the
afternoon—follow the four steps above.

Pick an English word. Learn the Spanish form of that
word. Practice it immediately.

Then ask "¿Suena bien?" to learn if you are pronouncing
it correctly.

> ### ¿SUENA BIEN?
> (**SWAY**-nah bee-**AYN**)
> Sound good?

Below is a simple "scripted loop" you can use to visualize,
plan, and practice engaging Spanish speakers with
¿Cómo se dice?

Scripted loops—once mastered within the context of
micro-fluency on a specific set of activities—allow you to
lead a conversation without having attained language
fluency.

Think of this looped script as a linguistic workflow,
mapping the probable path of a basic interaction on the
job. You simply start by finding someone who speaks
Spanish and asking him or her "¿Cómo se dice?" while
pointing at something. To the best of your ability, repeat

what that person says back to you. Then, to check the accuracy of your pronunciation, ask, "*¿Suena bien?*"

If you get a response indicating that, *yes*, your pronunciation sounds good, say **"OK, *excelente*. *Gracias*."** Which you probably already know means, "OK, excellent. Thanks."

If the feedback from the Spanish speaker is that your pronunciation was a bit off, that's when you start using the "looped" portion of this script. Simply jump back to the original question—"*¿Cómo se dice?*"—and repeat the process.

Here's a visual of how the scripted loop works:

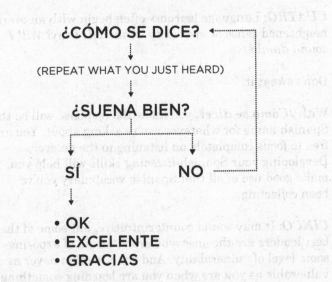

¿CÓMO SE DICE?

(REPEAT WHAT YOU JUST HEARD)

¿SUENA BIEN?

SÍ   **NO**

- **OK**
- **EXCELENTE**
- **GRACIAS**

Next, I will elaborate on this *¿Cómo se dice?* script, and later I'll provide two other examples of scripted loops that you can use confidently and immediately.

Capitalizing on *¿Cómo se dice?*

Beyond basic vocabulary building, there are five additional benefits to using *¿Cómo se dice?* on the job.

UNO: Every time you engage in conversation with a Spanish speaker, you gain more confidence in your own language skills.

DOS: When you bridge the language gap on the job, you connect with a Spanish speaker. You begin to develop a relationship, regardless of whether or not that was your intent.

TRES: With *¿Cómo se dice?*, *you* are in control. When you ask the question and listen to the response, you learn a new word that is relevant to *you*.

CUATRO: Language learners often begin with an overly heightened sense of insecurity. *What will I say? Will I sound dumb?*

Don't sweat it.

With *¿Cómo se dice?*, you know the response will be the Spanish name for whatever you're asking about. You are free to focus completely on listening to the answer. Developing your Spanish-*listening* skills will help you make good use of all that Spanish vocabulary you've been collecting.

CINCO: It may sound counterintuitive, but some of the best leaders are the ones who aren't afraid of exposing some level of vulnerability. And you are often never as vulnerable as you are when you are learning something new—especially a language.

Yes, you might stumble over your words—a lot.
But that's OK.

The more you try, the less you'll stumble.

Steve Brauer, group president at Zachry Industrial, a construction firm based in San Antonio, shared the following story with me after completing Red Angle's Safety Spanish program:

> *Recently, I walked up to a group of Spanish-speaking crafts people from our company, people I had never met before. It was a great chance to thank them for joining us and for allowing the president of the company to visit with them. I took the opportunity to tell them that I was a new student of Spanish, and then shared some of my learnings from the Safety Spanish program. They had fun with me and joked that "El Jefe" needed it for trips to Cancun! Everybody laughed and cut up and it made for a great employee "engagement victory."*

Part of the effectiveness of the *¿Cómo se dice?* script is that it places your average fluent Spanish speaker in the position of being the teacher, the authority, the imparter of knowledge. And when you place a Spanish speaker in such a role, even if only for a moment, you are making the person feel important.

The best leaders I've ever been around have been gifted at what I call **M**aking **O**ther **P**eople **F**eel **I**mportant, or **MOPFI**.

> **MOPFI**
> **M**ake **O**ther **P**eople **F**eel **I**mportant.

Don't underestimate the value of MOPFI. Don't underestimate the value of *¿Cómo se dice?* in MOPFI.

And don't underestimate your ability to become micro-fluent. It will help you solve on-the-job problems and build working relationships. And hey, it will even give you something unique to put on your LinkedIn profile.

And if we see each other at Starbucks, you will no doubt impress me when I politely eavesdrop on your *conversación*.

Watch your (emotional) bank account

In the classic book *The 7 Habits of Highly Effective People*, author Stephen Covey discusses the importance of managing your emotional bank account. Like any ordinary bank account, you need to make a deposit before you can make a withdrawal.

If you want to ask someone for a favor—a withdrawal— you will have a higher likelihood of getting what you want if you have already established trust, built rapport, or, at the very least, introduced yourself—made a deposit.

From discussing this concept in hundreds of workshops, I've found that even though this analogy makes intuitive sense with most people, executives and mid-managers still often ignore this basic emotional debit/credit concept with frontline workers who have different cultural and language preferences.

Managers often fail to make even the most fundamental of deposits—simply acknowledging Hispanic workers— on a daily basis and yet are surprised by the lack of cooperation when something goes wrong or someone gets hurt.

Sometimes this failure to make a deposit is a deliberate manifestation of the personal biases that can affect a manager's ability to lead. Other times it's merely human nature: we unconsciously navigate around or ignore potentially awkward situations . . .

Hmmm, are those eight Hispanic drywallers laughing about me right now? Or did I just happen to approach them at a time when they just happened to be laughing?

Hmmmm. I better look down and ignore them. Just keep walking and pretend to answer a call on your phone . . .

Regardless of where you fall on the spectrum of avoiding awkward situations, the result is the same. If we aren't making emotional deposits in advance, then when the time comes to solve problems and lead effectively there won't be anything to withdraw.

Risk-Free Emotional Deposits

To ensure we are keeping our bank accounts sufficiently stacked, we will now review four basic language exercises that can be easily remembered and deposited—and used immediately.

They're also (essentially) risk free.

Many managers and leaders—especially the ones who are *excelente*—are taught to assess risk constantly. It's no different when acquiring new language skills. The following simple phrases will allow you to connect with Spanish speakers in a casual, friendly manner—without the risk of an awkward situation.

1. Establish an introduction

A good introduction breaks the ice, engages the listener, and helps establish credibility. We will focus on five simple intros, a few of which you probably already know. By mastering these five introductory phrases, you can confidently begin piecing together your own script—those brief, daily conversations we discussed earlier that you can rehearse on the job.

We start with *Good morning* and *Good afternoon*. These introductions are respectful, simple, and universally acceptable ways to begin a conversation. Make note of the slight ending change between **buenos** for *Good morning* and **buenas** for *Good afternoon*.

BUENOS DÍAS.
(**BWAY**-nohs **DEE**-ahs)
Good morning.

BUENAS TARDES.
(**BWAY**-nahs **TAHR**-days)
Good afternoon.

Next we have a couple intros using *Cómo* ....

¿CÓMO ANDAS?
(**KOH**-moh **AHN**-dahs)
How's it going?

¿CÓMO ESTÁS?
(**KOH**-moh ay-**STAHS**)
How are you?

¿Cómo andas? is more casual than *Cómo estás* and will earn you a bit more street cred as well. Opt for this when speaking to a Hispanic drywaller who is 25.

The last intro is a simple, two-syllable phrase:

¿QÚE TAL?
(kay **TAHL**)
How's it going?

New Spanish-language learners don't use this last introduction very often, so it provides some different-iation. And with only two syllables, it's hard to screw up.

To keep things fresh, try to mix and match the introductions. If you know the name of the person you are speaking to, throw it in there as well.

- *Buenos días. ¿Cómo andas?*
- *Buenas tardes. ¿Qué tal?*
- *Buenos días, Pablo. ¿Cómo estás?*

The answer you'll hear most often—which you can also mimic—is the Spanish word for "good": *bien*. You will often hear that followed by the Spanish phrase *¿Y tú?* ("And you?"), which you can use as well.

> **BIEN**
> (bee-**AYN**)
> good, well

A simple conversation may start like this:

You: *Buenos días, Pablo. ¿Cómo estás?*
Pablo: *Sí, buenos días. Bien, gracias. ¿Y tú?*
You: *Bien, gracias.*

And with that, my friend, you are speaking Spanish. Master these five intros, and you'll make significant strides toward connecting with your fellow Hispanic co-workers—even with just a simple morning introduction.

2. Show appreciation

The philosopher and psychologist William James once said that "the deepest principle in human nature is the craving to be appreciated." Appreciation is indeed a universal characteristic, consistent across cultures. People like to be recognized for their efforts. So, let's do just that.

The easiest form of showing appreciation is to utilize the Spanish Twin *excelente*.

> **¡EXCELENTE!**
> (ayk-say-**LAYN**-tay)
> Excellent!

Here are two other brief phrases of appreciation to master:

> **MUY BIEN, GRACIAS.**
> (**MOOH**-ee bee-**AYN GRAH**-see-ahs)
> Very good, thanks.

> **BIEN HECHO, GRACIAS.**
> (bee-**AYN AY**-choh **GRAH**-see-ahs)
> Well done, thanks.

You can see that both of these phrases use *bien* ("good/well"). They also both use *gracias*, because saying thank you is a fundamental way to communicate appreciation in pretty much any language.

Keep in mind the *H* in *hecho* is silent, as are all *H*s in Spanish.

3. Model improvement

Your leadership skills hinge on your ability to coach for improved performance. Two words—*mira* and *mejor*—accompanied by a physical demonstration will allow you to instruct and coach workers across the language gap.

> **MIRA**
> (**MEE**-rah)
> look

> **MEJOR**
> (may-**HOHR**)
> better

The first step is to get your workers' attention with *mira*, as if to say, "Hey, guys, look over here." Next, act out the correct behavior you wish for them to model. For example, if you see a Hispanic worker lifting heavy boxes in a way that will surely strain his back, alert him with *mira* and then demonstrate the correct way to lift boxes by using your legs.

Stepping aside, you can motion with your hand to have the worker pick up the next box. When he models the new lifting method correctly, say *"Mejor."*

Mira and *mejor* are short, simple, and help you get right to the point. And the alliteration between the two words helps make this mini-script memorable.

4. Exit with an outro
There are dozens of ways to say, well, *adiós*. Here, we will focus on mastering two particular ways that can be used anywhere at any time.

> *¡NOS VEMOS!*
> (nohs **BAY**-mohs)
> We'll see ya!

> *HASTA LUEGO.*
> (**AH**-stah looh-**WAY**-goh)
> Until later!

Remember the Bince Baughn Rule of Pronunciation when learning the first one: all *V*s in Spanish sound like *B*s.

Armed with *Adiós*, *Hasta luego*, and *Nos vemos*, you can now confidently exit any *conversación* without having to resort to pretending to answer a call on your smartphone.

Risk-free emotional deposits

INTROS	APPRECIATION	IMPROVEMENT	OUTROS
¡Buenos días!	¡Excelente!	Mira . . . mejor.	Adiós
¡Buenas tardes!	Muy bien, gracias.	Como así.	Hasta luego.
¿Cómo estás?	Bien hecho, gracias.		Nos vemos.
¿Cómo andas?			OK excelente. Gracias.

IMPORTANTE Y OBVIO (IMPORTANT AND OBVIOUS)

There is one group of individuals on your jobsite ideally suited to helping you learn Spanish: bilinguals. All you have to do is ask. Let them know you are learning Spanish to become a better leader and would appreciate their help. More than likely, they will be impressed by your initiative and flattered you asked them.

Willpower is a limited resource. There will be times when you won't have the energy to engage in Spanish. So try enlisting the assistance of your bilingual colleagues.

They will help ensure you continue to build momentum, even when you don't feel like it.

The ¿Hay problemas? scripted loop

Earlier in this chapter, we revealed the first of our three scripted loops: *¿Cómo se dice?*

The second scripted loop we will review is the *¿Hay problemas?* loop. Our goal with this script is to connect with Spanish speakers while performing one of the most basic activities as a manager: identifying potential or existing problems and solving them to keep the job running safely and productively.

Asking "*¿Hay problemas?*" allows you to gather more information from workers on your jobsite. Before we say it together, remember, the *H* in Spanish is silent, and the "ay" in *hay* is pronounced like "eye." As for *problemas*, you no doubt already guessed that it's a Spanish Twin for "problems."

> **¿HAY PROBLEMAS?**
> (i proh-**BLAY**-mahs)
> Are there problems?

Upon asking "*¿Hay problemas?*" to your workers, if the feedback you receive is "*No, no hay problemas.*" ("No, there are no problems."), then you don't have a problem, and so you simply close out the conversation the same way we did in the *¿Cómo se dice?* loop: "**OK, excelente. Gracias.**"

However, if the feedback you receive—verbally or otherwise—is "*Sí, hay problemas,*" then, well, you *do* have a problem. If this happens, just say "*¿Dónde?*" ("Where?"). I know you still haven't quite mastered the Spanish language yet, so let's not make things harder on ourselves, OK? Avoid a lengthy response as to *why* something is wrong and just ask "*¿Dónde?*"

> **¿DÓNDE?**
> (**DOHN**-day)
> Where?

After seeing *el problema*, close out the conversation with "**OK, excelente. Gracias.**"

¿HAY PROBLEMAS?

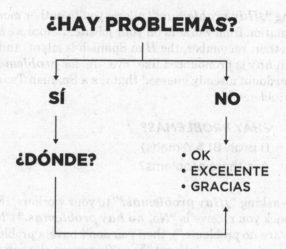

SÍ → ¿DÓNDE?

NO →
- OK
- EXCELENTE
- GRACIAS

The *¿Hay problemas?* loop is a tried-and-true method
for connecting with Hispanic workers and for gathering
information efficiently. Leveraging our Risk-Free
Emotional Deposits, a simple conversation can look
like this:

You: *Buenos días, Pablo. ¿Cómo estás?*
Pablo: *Sí, buenos días. Bien, gracias. ¿Y tú?*
You: *Bien, gracias. ¿Hay problemas?*
*Several Spanish sentences erupt, indicating there is an
issue with the insulation.*
You: *Hay problemas. OK. ¿Dónde?*
Pablo leads you around the corner to the obvious problem.
You: *Aha. OK, excelente. Gracias.*

Taking it a step further, you can leverage your knowledge
of *puede* ("can you") and Spanish Twins, such as *reparar*
("to repair") and *insulación* ("insulation").

You: *¿Puede reparar la insulación, Pablo?*
Pablo: *Sí. Puedo repararlo.* ("Yes. I can repair it.")
You: *Muy bien, Pablo. Muchas gracias.*

Master the fundamentals.
String them together.
Progress over perfection.

Everyone is from somewhere
The third and final script is the *¿De dónde eres?* script.

> ### *¿DE DÓNDE ERES?*
> (day **DOHN**-day **AY**-rays)
> Where are you from?

In sales, it is recommended you ask people where they are from instead of what they do—it typically makes for better conversation. For example, "I lived in New York City until I was 10 and then moved to Lexington, Kentucky," is significantly more fertile soil to till than "I'm in accounting."

Everyone is from somewhere, and our roots shape who we are and how we think. Hell, this whole book is about where people come from and how we can use that information to understand our workforce better so that we can lead more effectively.

The *¿De dónde eres?* script allows you to inquire about peoples' roots with planned conversational entry and exit points. As we know from Chapter 1, nearly 65 percent of Hispanics in the United States are from Mexico, and about 10 percent are from Puerto Rico. So we'll play the odds here and focus on these two countries.

The *¿De dónde eres?* script may appear daunting, but it's a docile beast and will consistently protect you as you forge new relationships *en español*. And it's arguably faster than other approaches given what we know about Hispanics. Because of their familial, collectivist nature, many Hispanics will have an easy time talking about their extended families—where they are from and how they stay connected. Expressing genuine interest in their roots and family is one of the fastest ways to build trust with someone.

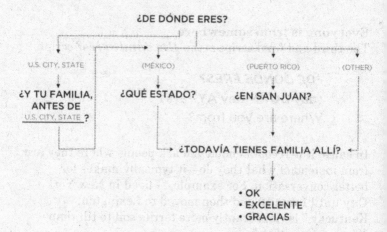

After asking **"¿De dónde eres?,"** don't be surprised if you hear the name of an American city. After all, Hispanic families have lived in the areas of Texas and California long before those regions became part of the United States. Furthermore, many Spanish speakers in the United States self-identify as Americans more than anything else. (Remember, also from Chapter 1: 67 percent of Hispanics of Mexican descent were *born in the United States*. For Hispanics of Puerto Rican descent, that number jumps all the way up to 98 percent.)

If the response you hear to **"¿De dónde eres?"** is, say, San Antonio or New York or some other American city, we want the speaker to go back even further in time, inclusive of their family.

¿Y TU FAMILIA, ANTES DE SAN ANTONIO?

(ee tooh fah-**MEE**-lee-ah **AHN**-tays day)

And your family, before San Antonio?

The answer to this question will get us back to playing the odds—that the speaker's roots are probably in Mexico or Puerto Rico.

If the answer is Mexico . . .
With just two words (when asked in sequence within this script), you can learn a lot more about the person you are speaking with—and quickly set yourself apart from your average manager.

> ### ¿QUÉ ESTADO?
> (kay ay-**STAH**-doh)
> What state?

Mexico is not merely a monolithic mass of indistinguishable civilization, and it's a far cry from the commonly held stereotype of raucous spring breakers in Cancún or Cabo downing tequila shots at places like Señor Frog's.

There's a rich and complex history behind Mexico and all of its 31 states and one federal district. And that history is matched by an equally rich culture and a proud people. Just as there is a great difference between Montana and Massachusetts, there's an equally great difference between Chiapas and Chihuahua.

By asking "*¿Qué estado?*," you are peeling back the onion more than your average person usually does and showing a genuine interest in the Hispanic person's roots you are inquiring about.

After learning which specific state within Mexico this speaker's family is from, you'll peel the onion back even further by asking if the speaker still has family there.

> ### ¿TODAVÍA TIENES FAMILIA ALLÍ?
> (toh-dah-**BEE**-ah tee-**AY**-nays fah-**MEE**-lee-ah ah-**YEE**)
> Still have family there?

More often than not, you'll hear some version of *Sí*, with some additional information. At this point in the exchange, you can simply close out the conversation by employing our old standby, *"OK, excelente. Gracias.,"* which we used in the *¿Hay Problemas?* and *¿Como se dice?* scripted loops.

If the answer is Puerto Rico . . .

Again, we'll play the odds here. San Juan (if you're curious about the translation, it's St. John) is the capital of Puerto Rico and the largest of the commonwealth's 78 municipalities by a factor of at least two. Four of the five next largest municipalities are adjacent to San Juan. Nearly 30 percent of Puerto Ricans live in or next to San Juan, so we'll ask the following question:

> **¿EN SAN JUAN?**
> (ayn sahn **HWAHN**)
> In San Juan?

Proceed by asking the same question we did for Spanish speakers with Mexican roots: *"¿Todavía tienes familia allí?"* Then follow with the closing, *"OK, excelente. Gracias."*

For all others . . .

If playing the odds failed here and you heard another country (recall from Chapter 1, the next most popular countries will be Cuba, El Salvador, the Dominican Republic, and Colombia), skip to *"¿Todavía tienes familia allí?"*

Hispanic workers rarely receive this type of curiosity from English-speaking managers, so by following this script you'll be differentiating yourself immediately. Doing so will demonstrate genuine interest and will enable you more quickly to establish trust—the underpinning for all leadership and performance improvement.

> **QUICK STATUS CHECK**
> By this point, you've learned several (168, to be exact)
> Spanish Twins, many of which should be useful on the
> job. You've learned that retention is easy when the
> content you are learning is relevant, entertaining, and
> brief. You're seeing Spanish all over the place now—
> from the names of new cars to the towns in your state.
> And most recently, we've dissected what micro-fluency
> looks like, with the targeted mastery of Risk-Free
> Emotional Deposits (Establish an introduction, Show
> appreciation, Model improvement, and Exit with an
> outro) and three specific scripted loops.

What's the frequency, Kenneth?

The final piece of the micro-fluency puzzle is Frequency.
Author Tim Ferriss (the minimum-effective-dose guy)
offers a practical view on the importance of studying the
right things—in our case, studying the most frequently
used terms that are relevant to our business.

> *If you select the wrong material, it does not matter
> how you study or if you study—practical fluency is
> impossible without the proper tools (material);
> teachers are subordinate to materials, just as
> cooks are subordinate to recipes.*

The early 1990s was a defining period in my life. My
hometown Chicago Bulls, led by Michael Jordan, Scotty
Pippen, and Phil Jackson, were establishing a dynasty.
The movie *Pulp Fiction* blew my mind in ways a movie
hadn't before. The music of R.E.M.—specifically their
Monster album, with the opening track, "What's the
Frequency, Kenneth?"—has remained locked in my
cerebral cortex for good.

Also during this period is when I remember learning my
first new Spanish word in a classroom setting: *piscina*.

PISCINA
(pee-**SEE**-nah)
pool

I don't know why this specific word has stayed with me for so long. Perhaps it's the linguistic equivalent of a first crush. Whatever the reason, *piscina* has always held a special place in my heart and mind. Yet as often happens with the various short-lived obsessions of our youth, I later learned that *piscina* wasn't all it was cracked up to be.

When studying in Guadalajara, Mexico, years later in college, I learned they actually use another term: *alberca*.

ALBERCA
(ahl-**BAYR**-kah)
pool

Piscina is used in Spain.
Alberca is used Mexico.

This was annoying. Here I had committed to memory a term that was inherently useless in my daily existence. No one who lived near me and spoke Spanish would ever say *piscina*. Now I had to unlearn *piscina* and make room in my mind for *alberca*.

I was determined not to waste my foreign-language capital like this ever again.

As a Spanish major in college, I realized that the courses I was taking were preparing me for how to teach high-school Spanish. Regardless of how I *actually* wanted to end up applying my Spanish skills, this was the broad, catch-all train I'd jumped on.

Searching for more practical, real-world content to focus on instead (think *alberca*, not *piscina*), I asked my program advisor what the easiest way was to identify the most commonly spoken and written words in the Spanish language. I wanted to trade in *piscina* for something a bit more . . . practical.

"You mean a list of the most frequently used words in Spanish?" she asked.

"Yes!" I said excitedly. "That's exactly what I want. Any ideas on how I can start compiling that?"

She looked at me funny.

"Well, I'd save some time and just buy a frequency dictionary in Spanish," she said, smiling. "No need to reinvent *la rueda*, Hartmann."

I was pissed.

I'd been studying Spanish for *six* years, and this was the first time anyone had mentioned anything about a "frequency dictionary." Not only should every Spanish student know about this tool, I recommended to my advisor, every class should require its usage.

A frequency dictionary in Spanish, I reasoned, would be the living embodiment of the 80/20 rule—that 20 percent of the effort results in 80 percent of the reward. Applying this to the Spanish language, 20 percent of all the words in Spanish would probably account for 80 percent of all the words *spoken* in Spanish, right?

I was way off.
Turns out, it's even less—way less.

Tim Ferriss has the real math behind Spanish fluency:

> To be perceived as fluent in conversational Spanish, for example, you need an active vocabulary of approx-imately 2,500 high-frequency words. This will allow

*you to comprehend more than 95% of all conversation.
To get to 98% comprehension would require at least five
years of practice instead of five months. Doing the
math, 2,500 words is a mere 2.5% of the estimated
100,000 words in the Spanish language.*

*This means: 2.5% of the total subject matter provides
95% of the desired results. This same 2.5% provides
just 3% less benefit than putting in 12 times as much
effort.*

This is the basis behind the MED, the minimum effective
dose, and why identifying the most frequently used words
is so critical.

I immediately purchased the Spanish frequency
dictionary. With anticipation, I flipped to the index at the
back of the book. I wanted to start my frequency
exploration with one Spanish word in particular.

And there it was . . . **piscina**. The 4,653rd most
frequently used word in Spanish[1]. People often speak
of learning disabilities. This was a perfect example of a
teaching disability. I was perfectly capable of *learning*
the right word—I just wasn't *taught* the right word.

From frequency to (micro) fluency
Examining the list of the 40 most frequently used words
in Spanish on the following page, you should quickly
notice that none of the top 10 words has more than three
letters.

Like English, the most common words are the small ones
that effectively connect our thoughts into coherent
sentences.

Ten of the top 40 are verbs. As a Spanish major, I had to
engage in rote memorization of all 14 grammatical ways
to conjugate these verbs.

As you may have guessed by now, this is largely unnecessary to speak conversationally on the job.

In Red Angle's Construction Conversational program (an intermediate-level class), for example, we focus on some key phrases in the present, past, and future tenses, along with some top-40 high-frequency terms and key nouns specific to the jobsite.

In short order, construction managers are engaging in conversations (micro) fluently. Remember the manager from the beginning of this chapter who claimed to be fluent in Landscape Spanish? When I inquired about his language-learning process, he said he started slowly. He learned a few introductions first and then created a brief list of the most common words he needed to know. Once he became confident with his landscape-specific vocabulary list, he began asking his bilingual foreman for help building short sentences. Then he practiced these sentences daily.

It didn't happen overnight, he said, but within a few months he was providing guidance and asking questions to his landscaping crews entirely in Spanish. This is micro-fluency.

1	el/la (def.art.) the
2	de (prep.) of, from
3	que (conj.) that, which
4	y (conj.) and
5	a (prep.) to, at
6	en (prep.) in, on
7	un (indef. art.) a, an
8	ser (verb) to be
9	se (pron.) -self, oneself
10	no (adv.) no
11	haber (verb) to have
12	por (prep.) by, for, through
13	con (prep.) with
14	su (adj.) his, her, their, your
15	para (prep.) for, to, in order to
16	como (conj.) like, as
17	estar (verb) to be
18	tener (verb) to have
19	le (pron.)
20	lo (art.) the (+noun)
21	lo (pron.) it
22	todo (adj.) all, every
23	pero (conj.) but, yet, except
24	más (adj.) more
25	hacer (verb) to do, make
26	o (conj.) or
27	poder (verb) to be able to, can
28	decir (verb) to tell, say
29	este (adj.) this (m); esta (f)
30	ir (verb) to go
31	otro (adj.) other, another
32	ese (adj.) that (m); esa (f)
33	la (pron.)
34	si (conj.) if, whether
35	me (pron.) me
36	ya (adv.) already, still
37	ver (verb) to see
38	porque (conj.) because
39	dar (verb) to give
40	cuando (conj.) when

Progress over perfection

Business coach Dan Sullivan articulates a critical aspect of improving at anything in life. Sullivan notes in his book, *Learning to Avoid the Gap: The skill of Building Lifetime Happiness*, that many high achievers have low self-esteem and are extremely hard on themselves, despite their considerable achievements.

From his work with thousands of entrepreneurs, he identified a gap between where individuals were starting from and where they wanted to go—their *ideal self*.

As these individuals began their path toward improving themselves—much like you have started to do by reading this book—instead of focusing on their progress, they continued to measure themselves against their ideal self.

In working with Red Angle clients, I see this behavior a lot. Participants will often say to me, dejectedly, "I'm still a long way from fluent." And this is after finishing our six-week program that requires only ten minutes of study a day.

My instinct is to say, "Well, no shit."
And sometimes I do.

But usually I just say, "Give it some time."

When I ask participants about their progress, they often share stories about the excitement they feel from solving problems with even the little Spanish they now know. I hear the chuckles that ride shotgun to the stories of eliminating the small daily frustrations about cleanup or lockup at the end of a long day.

Anyone beginning down the path of language acquisition will surely fantasize about the ideal—imagining themselves fluently speaking Spanish to co-workers while bosses and subordinates alike exchange glances of amazement.

That's the ideal.
And it's OK to daydream about for a bit.
But then come back down to reality.

Measure backward, not forward.

Measure your progress from where you started from and where you are now. Measure *progress*, not the ideal. Keep in mind you're playing the long game, continually improving a day at a time.

As humans, we tend to overestimate what we can do in a day or a week or a month, but severely underestimate what we are capable of in a year or 18 months or a decade.

You don't need a full college course in Spanish to be able to relate to and communicate with the Hispanic members of your workforce. With just a modest amount of effort to study and learn the practical, functional information and exercises in this book, you can significantly improve your leadership skills on the job and take your level of management from good to *excelente*.

C

Closing

GOOD TO *EXCELENTE* FRAMEWORK™

AWARENESS OF CULTURE

| RECOGNIZE + ACCEPT *LA REALIDAD* | UNDERSTAND THE ORIGINS | DISTINGUISH AMONG THE DIMENSIONS |

AWARENESS OF LANGUAGE

| SECRET OF THE SPANISH TWINS | EMBRACE THE EQUATION | FORWARD WITH (MICRO) FLUENCY |

Man does not simply exist but always decides what his existence will be, what he will become the next moment. By the same token, every human being has the freedom to change at any instant.

—*Viktor Frankl*

Demography is destiny

Over the next three decades, the United States is expected to host a population of roughly 400 million people. To those already wary of the negative side effects of densely populated areas, this news might seem worrisome. Joel Kotkin, author and urban studies fellow at Chapman University, in Orange, California, however, is optimistic. In his book *The Next Hundred Million: America in 2050*, he writes, "because of America's unique demographic trajectory among advanced countries, it should emerge by midcentury as the most affluent, culturally rich, and successful nation in human history." [1]

While global powers in Europe and Asia grapple with the national effects of population decline, the United States faces robust population growth, led in large part by Hispanics. This steady demographic increase has broad implications for governments and businesses alike—not to mention the very citizens of this country. Individuals and organizations that acknowledge, accept, and adapt to this changing face of America will be best suited to work with and lead it.

I feel blessed to have been born in this great country and I am undoubtedly and unabashedly optimistic about the future—or *el futuro*.

Others around you—colleagues, bosses, friends, neighbors, family—might be less optimistic. They may view this growth with pessimism or fear. And that is understandable.

Change can be uncomfortable.

As Mark Twain put it, "The only person who likes change is a wet baby."

I challenge that statement, though.
We actively sign up for change all the time.

We change jobs.
We get married.
We buy new homes.
We move to different states.
We have children.

These are all big changes in our lives that we willingly (for the most part) sign up for. Change is part of living.

But who am I to disagree with Twain?

Let's just say I lean toward another quote regarding change. It's from four-star general and former U.S. Army chief of staff Eric Shinseki: "If you don't like change, you are going to like irrelevance even less."

Demography, it is often said, is destiny. If you plan on living in the United States for the next few decades, you're signing up for change. And if you don't recognize that reality, you risk getting left behind.

As you apply the cultural and language concepts in this book to expand your leadership capabilities, expect resistance. Many around you will want to hang onto the status quo for as long as possible.

Listen empathetically.
Ask questions.
Build trust.

And don't forget to mention that history has a way of repeating itself.

From Dillingham to willing and able
Have you heard about the Dillingham Commission? In response to continued pressure among American citizens to evaluate immigration in the United States, Congress and the Senate green-lit a study led by a senator from Vermont named William P. Dillingham.

Following a four-year, state-by-state analysis of immigration, the study—known as the Dillingham Commission—revealed its findings. Chief among them was the consensus that the new wave of immigrants arriving in the United States was different from previous generations of immigrants in how they assimilated to their new country.

The earlier immigrants came to the United States and mixed well with their new surroundings. They had unique skills. They accepted the American culture. They learned English quickly. They . . . "mingled." In short, they assimilated quickly.

But those days, the commission found, were over. The new wave of immigrants were increasingly unskilled laborers, insulated within their communities from much-needed assimilation. Many continued to use their native language while in the United States.

To correct course, the committee urged lawmakers to support new legislation. Among the recommendations, lawmakers should "look especially to the economic well-being of our people," further restrict unskilled immigrants, and implement a mandatory literacy test for immigrants.

Despite the seemingly constant conversation about immigration recently, you likely missed the Dillingham Commission's report. That's because it was completed more than a century ago, in 1910, and focused on immigrants arriving in the 1880s from Europe.[2]

This isn't a new conversation.
History repeats itself.
It's a cycle.

Our *bracero* mentality

There is a recurring theme in American history: When the economy is good, we roll out the welcome mat to immigrant labor for economic growth and capitalistic gain. When the economy turns for the worse, we blame immigrants, call them job thieves, and increase deportations.

The economy is cyclical. Historically, Americans' treatment of immigrants has been cyclical as well.

For example, in the early 1900s, as America's infrastructure was being constructed, millions of Hispanics—predominantly Mexicans—were welcomed into the country, filling the existing labor shortage ably.

Then, in the 1930s, as the Great Depression was gripping America, President Herbert Hoover, citing the stealing of American jobs, deported hundreds of thousands of these immigrants "back to Mexico." The only problem was that by then, roughly half of them were American citizens, having lived in Arizona, New Mexico, Colorado, Nevada, and California for decades. (Remember that Absolut Vodka map from Chapter 2? This land belonged to Mexico until 1848, when residents of these territories became U.S. citizens.)

Many of the Mexican Americans being deported had never set foot in Mexico. A lot of them didn't even speak Spanish.

Not too many years later, the cycle would continue.

During World War II, American farmers faced a severe labor shortage. As greater numbers of men were being drafted into the military, farms were left without enough workers to harvest the country's crops—which were in high demand. As a result, food was left rotting in the fields. Uncle Sam stepped in and paid the Mexican government for a few million strong backs to help solve the problem. This was known as the Bracero Program.

Millions of Mexicans boarded trains and worked to help feed their northern neighbors during the war. The Bracero (Spanish for "manual laborer") Program was the largest guest-worker program in American history.[3]

Then the war ended.
And a recession hit.
How did the American government respond?

President Dwight D. Eisenhower quietly rolled out *Operation Wetback* (yes, really) and deported thousands of Mexicans.

Decades later, from 1990 to 2007, Hispanics were once again welcomed into the country, their labor being instrumental to the growth of the U.S. economy. But when the Great Recession hit, President Obama, following in the footsteps of his presidential predecessors, deported thousands.

The economy is cyclical. Historically, Americans' treatment of immigrants has been cyclical as well.

Our Bracero Mentality—welcoming Hispanic labor in the good times, deporting during recessions—hinders our long-term stability as a nation of growth, both culturally and economically. Among Hispanics, this history of treatment is passed down through the generations. The Smithsonian Institution, in telling the *bracero* story through a traveling exhibition, said it best: "Both bitter and sweet, the *bracero* experience tells a story of opportunity, but also of exploitation."[4]

No, you can't change history.
And no, you can't guarantee the future.

You can, however, study the present context and understand how it drives the attitude and behavior of the Hispanic worker. For those individuals and firms that do, their cultural differentiation will be immediately apparent—and they will be best positioned to jump from good to great to *excelente*.

The Golden Rule is wrong

In every culture and language on Earth, some version of the Golden Rule exists. The gist of it is this: Treat others as you would like to be treated.

But could the Golden Rule be . . . wrong?

Knowing what you know now about different cultures, can you see how the Golden Rule might not apply in *all* situations?

Different cultures view the world differently. If we base our treatment of others solely on how *we* would like to be treated, we are making one big assumption: *they think like we do*.

We need to remove ourselves from the equation. It's about *them*, not us.

The question then becomes, "How would *they* like to be treated?"

We should strive to treat others as *they* would like to be treated. To do that, we need to ask better questions, listen more closely, and live with more empathy—through our actions and our words.

Empathy, the ability to understand and share the feelings of another person, is a critical skill to master and one that will help you adjust your leadership style as needed to build more trust with those around you.

Meg Bear, a long-time executive at high-growth Silicon Valley firms, believes "empathy is the critical 21st-century skill." She calls it the skill "I need to develop in myself, my teams, and my children" and concludes that "empathy will be the difference between good and great." [5]

And between great and *excelente*.

I wish you luck on your journey.
Thanks for reading.

¡Muchísimas gracias!

Writing a book is hardly a solo adventure. I'd like to
say muchísimas gracias to the following people. This
book would not be possible without their
commitment, expertise, and most of all—their
patience with me. To my wife, Melissa, who played
the roles of editor, proofreader, fact checker, and
psychiatrist over the past two years. Without her
ability to patiently listen and support me during this
process, G2E would never have made it to print. To
my sons, Brayden & Redding, who tolerated my
frequent weekend disappearing acts to write. Their
flexibility, cheerfulness, and endless hugs reduced
the guilt of this quasi-absentee parent. To my in-
laws, Sandra Meana, who logged dozens of extra
hours watching the boys, and Fernando Meana, who
willingly answered my endless series of questions
about his youth in Cuba and his experiences as a
Peter Pan kid. I owe a debt of gratitude to all our
Red Angle clients. If you're lucky in business, you get
to work with individuals you respect, admire, and
enjoy being around while achieving results. I have
learned so much from our collaborations. Without a
doubt, I have been very lucky. To Rich Horwath, who
has been a generous mentor. His advice and
guidance has been profound. Thanks for everything.
To Professor James Jenkins, Dr. Heather Yates, and
Professor Garry Kroft and all their students at
Purdue University, Oklahoma State University, and
the University of Wisconsin-Stout, respectively.
Their enthusiasm—even at 7:30 am on Friday
mornings—consistently energizes me and improves
my ability to see the world through a different lens.
To Drew Holzfeind, whose editing skills improved
the quality of this book by a factor of 13. His
fingerprints are all over every chapter in this book
and his sense of humor made even the most stressful
parts of this editing process enjoyable. Drew is a true
talent.

To Joe Reed, who designed this book, inside and out. Joe's tolerance for my OCD tendencies was astounding. To Todd Withrow and his team at Niche Labs who designed the front cover and Zoë Foote, whose fact-checking, citation skills, and research was a great help. To Meloni McDaniel, whose willingness to think differently and lead in a new ways is both inspiring and motivating. To Marco Villasana, Steve Brauer, Ladd Henley, and Ana-María Phillips, who graciously allowed me to share our personal conversations with a much larger audience. Thank you all—*muchísimas gracias*.

E

Endnotes

GOOD TO *EXCELENTE* FRAMEWORK™

AWARENESS OF CULTURE

| RECOGNIZE + ACCEPT *LA REALIDAD* | UNDERSTAND THE ORIGINS | DISTINGUISH AMONG THE DIMENSIONS |

AWARENESS OF LANGUAGE

| SECRET OF THE SPANISH TWINS | EMBRACE THE EQUATION | FORWARD WITH (MICRO) FLUENCY |

INTRODUCCIÓN ENDNOTES

1. An expatriate is someone who lives outside his or her native country.

2. David Rennie, "How to fire up America," *Economist*, March 14, 2015, http://www.economist.com/news/leaders/21646202-rise-latinos-huge-opportunity-united-states-must-not-squander-it-how-fire-up.

3. Stephen Burgen, "US now has more Spanish speakers than Spain – only Mexico has more," *Guardian*, June 29, 2015, http://www.theguardian.com/us-news/2015/jun/29/us-second-biggest-spanish-speaking-country.

4. Nielsen Insights, "Hispanic Influence Reaches New Heights in the U.S.," Nielson.com, August 23, 2016, http://www.nielsen.com/us/en/insights/news/2016/hispanic-influence-reaches-new-heights-in-the-us.html.

5. Robert W. Fairlie, Arnobio Morelix, E.J. Reedy, and Joshua Russell, *The 2016 Kauffman Index of Startup Activity: National Trends*, Ewing Marion Kauffman Foundation, August 2016, www.kauffman.org/~/media/kauffman_org/microsites/kauffman_index/startup_activity_2016/kauffman_index_startup_activity_national_trends_2016.pdf.

CHAPTER 1 ENDNOTES

1. The term *Hispanic* made its official debut on the U.S. census form in 1980.

2. Mark Hugo Lopez, "Hispanic or Latino? Many don't care, except in Texas," Pew Research Center, October 28, 2013, www.pewresearch.org/fact-tank/2013/10/28/in-texas-its-hispanic-por-favor.

3. Yes, Mexico is in North America. Think of NAFTA, the North American Free Trade Agreement, whose members are Canada, the United States, and . . . Mexico.

4. The United States Census Bureau, accessed February 22, 2017. www.census.gov/topics/population/hispanic-origin.html.

5. Ana Gonzalez-Barrera, "More Mexicans Leaving Than Coming to the U.S.," Pew Research Center, November 19, 2015, http://www.pewhispanic.org/2015/11/19/more-mexicans-leaving-than-coming-to-the-u-s.

6. A curious one, aren't you? Fine then. If you must know, the mode is the number that appears most frequently in a data set.

7. Farhad Manjoo, "Walmart's evolution from big box giant to e-commerce innovator," *Fast Company*, November 26, 2012, www.fastcompany.com/3002948/walmarts-evolution-big-box-giant-e-commerce-innovator.

8. Jens Manuel Krogstad, Ana Gonzalez-Barrera, and Mark Hugo Lopez, "Children 12 and under are fastest growing group of unaccompanied minors at U.S. border," Pew Research Center, July 22, 2014, www.pewresearch.org/fact-tank/2014/07/22/children-12-and-under-are-fastest-growing-group-of-unaccompanied-minors-at-u-s-border.

9. See Jeff Asher, "U.S. cities experienced another big rise in murder in 2016," FiveThirtyEight, January 9, 2017, https://fivethirtyeight.com/features/u-s-cities-experienced-another-big-rise-in-murder-in-2016; and Robert Muggah, "It's official: San Salvador is the murder capital of the world," *Los Angeles Times*, March 2, 2016, http://www.latimes.com/opinion/op-ed/la-oe-0302-muggah-el-salvador-crime-20160302-story.html.

10. See *Transnational Organized Crime in Central America and the Caribbean: A Threat Assessment*, United Nations Office on Drugs and Crime, September 2012, http://www.unodc.org/documents/data-and-analysis/Studies/TOC_Central_America_and_the_Caribbean_english.pdf; and *Global Study on Homicide 2013: Trends, Contexts, Data*, United Nations Office on Drugs and Crime, March 2014, http://www.unodc.org/documents/gsh/pdfs/2014_GLOBAL_HOMICIDE_BOOK_web.pdf.

11. Katherine Rosenberg-Douglas and Tony Briscoe, "2016 ends with 762 homicides; 2017 opens with fatal Uptown gunfight,"

Chicago Tribune, January 2, 2017, http://www.chicago
tribune.com/news/local/breaking/ct-two-shot-to-death-in-
uptown-marks-first-homicide-of-2017-20170101-story.html.

12. Neal Holladay, *Working with Hispanics*, Hispanic Business
Nevada, www.hispanicbusinessnevada.com/wp-
content/uploads/WorkingwithHispanics.pdf.

CHAPTER 2 ENDNOTES

1. This quote is attributed to José de la Cruz Porfirio Díaz Mori,
the 29th president of Mexico (1884–1911).

2. World Development Indicators database, World Bank,
February 2017, http://databank.worldbank.org/
data/download/GDP.pdf.

3. *The World Factbook*, Central Intelligence Agency, January
2017, https://www.cia.gov/library/publications/resources/the-
world-factbook/geos/mx.html.

4. *The Global Competitiveness Report 2016–2017*, World
Economic Forum, September 2016, https://www.weforum.org
/reports/the-global-competitiveness-report-2016-2017-1.

5 Roderic Ai Camp, *Mexico: What Everyone Needs to Know*, New
York, NY: Oxford University Press, 2011.

6. William H. Beezley and Michael C. Meyer, eds, *The Oxford
History of Mexico*, New York, NY: Oxford University Press,
2010.

7. Mario Vargas Llosa, "México es la dictadura perfecta," *El
País*, September 1, 1990.

8. Lawrence Weiner, "How Mexico Became so Corrupt," *Atlantic*,
June 25, 2013, https://www.theatlantic.com/
international/archive/2013/06/how-mexico-became-so-
corrupt/277219/.

9. President Enrique Peña Nieto denationalized PEMEX in 2014
in an effort to increases investment in the country and improve
profitability. His timing was poor as the price of oil began its
free fall around the same time.

10. Andrew V. Pestano, "Mexican President Penna Nieto apologizes for $7 million corruption scandal, " United Press International, July 19 2016, http://www.upi.com/Top_News/World-News/2016/07/19/Mexican-President-Pea-Nieto-apologizes-for-7-million-corruption-scandal/8601468932469/.

11. Azam Ahmed & Randal C. Archibold, "Mexican Drug Kingpin, El Chapo, Escapes Prison Through Tunnel," New York Times, July 12, 2015, https://www.nytimes.com/2015/07/13/world/americas/joaquin-guzman-loera-el-chapo-mexican-drug-kingpin-prison-escape.html.

12. Azam Ahmed, "El Chapo, Mexican Drug Kingpin, Is Extradited to U.S.," New York Times, January 19, 2017, https://www.nytimes.com/2017/01/19/world/el-chapo-extradited-mexico.html.

13. Ioan Grillo, El Narco: Behind Mexico's Criminal Insurgency, New York, NY: Bloomsbury Publishing USA, 2011.

14. James Surowiecki, "The Puerto Rican Problem," New Yorker, April 6, 2015, http://www.newyorker.com/magazine/2015/04/06/the-puerto-rican-problem.

15. The World Factbook, Central Intelligence Agency, January 12, 2017, https://www.cia.gov/library/publications/the-world-factbook/geos/rq.html.

16. Ray Suarez, Latino Americans: The 500-Year Legacy That Shaped a Nation, New York, NY: Penguin Group, 2013.

17. Sam Erman, "Meanings of Citizenship in the U.S. Empire: Puerto Rico, Isabel Gonzalez, and the Supreme Court, 1898 to 1905," Journal of American Ethnic History, Vol. 27 No. 4, Summer 2008, https://www.researchgate.net/publication/242249414_Meanings_of_Citizenship_in_the_US_Empire_Puerto_Rico_Isabel_Gonzalez_and_the_Supreme_Court_1898_to_1905.

18. He surely caught hell for that at the dinner table for the rest of his life. "Oh sure, you can persuade the butcher to give you a deal on this leg of lamb, but could you persuade your shift supervisor to give you two hours to help me get in this country? Noooooooo . . . Increíble, Juan Francisco Torres!"

19. Suarez, *Latino Americans*.

20. *Boricua* refers to a native of Borinquen—the island of Puerto Rico's original name.

21. When the United States took control of Puerto Rico following the Treaty of Paris, the island's name was changed to *Porto Rico*, presumably to match the spelling to the American pronunciation. I find the arrogance here to be nothing short of stunning. *Puerto Rico* returned in 1932.

22. Victoria Burnett, "Amid Grim Economic Forecasts, Cubans Fear a Return to Darker Times," *New York Times*, July 12, 2016, https://www.nytimes.com/2016/07/13/world/americas/cuba-economy-venezuela-power-cuts.html.

23. "The Bay of Pigs Invasion," Central Intelligence Agency, April 18, 2016, https://www.cia.gov/news-information/featured-story-archive/2016-featured-story-archive/the-bay-of-pigs-invasion.html.

24. "The Bay of Pigs," John F. Kennedy Presidential Library and Museum, accessed December 5, 2016, https://www.jfklibrary.org/JFK/JFK-in-History/The-Bay-of-Pigs.aspx.

25. Anthony Boadle, "Castro: Cuba not cashing US Guantanamo rent checks," *Reuters*, August 17, 2007, www.reuters.com/article/idUSN17200921.

26. "History: The Cuban Children's Exodus," Operation Pedro Pan Group, Inc., accessed May 15, 2016, http://www.pedropan.org/ category/history.

27. Amy Chua and Jed Rubenfeld, *The Triple Package: How Three Unlikely Traits Explain the Rise and Fall of Cultural Groups in America*, New York, NY: Penguin, 2014.

28. Rick Sanchez, "Rick Sanchez: Cubans, an immigrant success model," Fox News, September 18, 2014, http://www.foxnews.com/opinion/2014/09/18/rick-sanchez-cubans-immigrant-success-model.html.

29. Ibid.

30. El Salvador is roughly the same size as New Jersey.

31. Duncan Currie, "The Bad and the Good in El Salvador," *National Review*, March 24, 2011, http://www.national review.com/corner/262979/bad-and-good-el-salvador-duncan-currie.

32. "Decretan cárcel para expresidente Saca," *Contra Punto*, November 5, 2016, http://contrapunto.com .sv/sociedad/judicial/decretan-carcel-para-expresidente-saca/2112.

33. Eric Ching, "In Search of the Party: The Communist Party, the Comintern, and the Peasant Rebellion of 1932 in El Salvador," *The Americas*, Vol. 55, No. 2, 1998, pp. 204–239. www.jstor.org/stable/1008053.

34. Workplace productivity had to be nil during this time.

35. Alain Rouquié and Michel Vale, "Honduras – El Salvador, The War of One Hundred Hours: A Case of Regional Disintegration," *International Journal of Politics*, Vol. 3, No. 3, 1973, pp. 17–51, www.jstor.org/stable/27868774.

36. Trucha (TROOH-chah) also means trout, as in the fish. As for the name Mara, it supposedly stems from the Spanish translation of a Charlton Heston movie from 1954 that was a hit in El Salvador, *The Naked Jungle*. Go figure.

37. "The MS-13 Threat: A National Assessment," The Federal Bureau of Investigation, January 14, 2008, https://archives.fbi.gov/archives/news/stories/2008/january/ms13 _011408.

38. "Joya de Cerén: Ruins in Around San Salvador," Lonely Planet, accessed June 5, 2016, https://www.lonelyplanet.com/el-salvador/around-san-salvador/attractions/joya-de-ceren/a/poi-sig/1337361/1328358.

39. *Building a Better Future Together: Dominican Republic Policy Notes*, World Bank Group, 2016, https://openknowledge.worldbank.org/handle/10986/26045.

40. *The World Factbook*, Central Intelligence Agency, January 12, 2017, https://www.cia.gov/library/publications/the-world-factbook/geos/dr.html.

41. Augusto Sención Villalona, *La dictadura de Trujillo (1930–1961)*, Archivo General de la Nación, Vol. 183, Santo Domingo 2012.

42. Grupo Puntacana Fundación, *Get Involved*. Accessed August 2, 2016. http://www.puntacana.org/to-do/voluntarism.

CHAPTER 3 ENDNOTES

1. I mean, the right to bear arms.

2. Geert Hofstede, Gert van Hofstede, and Michael Minkov, *Cultures and Organizations: Software of the Mind*, McGraw-Hill Education, May 2010.

3. Ibid.

4. Geert Hofstede, *National Culture*. Accessed May 4, 2016. https://www.geert-hofstede.com/national-culture.html.

5. Ibid.

6. Did slave-owning founding fathers embrace the hypocrisy here—or simply ignore it?

7. Or a lot. Raúl Salinas, brother of former Mexican president Carlos Salinas, was found to have amassed $114 million in British and Swiss bank accounts. That's a lot of penny pinching for a career government employee.

8. While everyone believes this quote to be from Lombardi, UCLA Bruins football coach Henry Russell "Red" Sanders was quoted as saying it first.

9. Hofstede, *Cultures and Organizations*.

10. Ibid.

11. Xiuwen Sue Dong, DrPH; Xuanwen Wang, PhD, Rebecca Katz, MPH, Gavin West, MPH, Jessica Bunting, MPH, *Fall Injuries and Prevention in the Construction Industry Q1 2017*, The Center for Construction Research and Training, http://www.cpwr.com/sites/default/files/publications/Quarter1-QDR-2017.pdf.

12. Stephen M. R. Covey, *The Speed of Trust: The One Thing that Changes Everything*, New York, NY: Free Press, 2008.

13. Erin Meyer, *The Culture Map: Breaking Through the Invisible Boundaries of Global Business*, New York, NY: Public Affairs Publishing, 2014.

14. Christine Romans and Patrick Gillespie, "Mexico gets more cash from its workers abroad than from oil," *CNN Money*, September 1, 2016, http://money.cnn.com/2016/09/01/news/economy/mexico-peso-money-transfer-trump-remittance.

15. David Livermore, *Leading with Cultural Intelligence: The Real Secret to Success*, New York, NY: AMACOM, 2015.

16. If you are a Cowboys fan, go easy on me here—and on Tony, for that matter. Quarterback is the toughest position to play in professional sports. As a life-long Chicago Bears fan, lemme tell you—without a decent QB, it can always get worse. Our last Pro Bowl signal caller was Jim McMahon, the "punky QB." In 1985.

17. Although the metal sign near the bathroom on which this story appeared claimed the author to be unknown, this is most likely an adaptation of an original story by German writer Heinrich Böll titled *Anekdote zur Senkung der Arbeitsmoral* ("Anecdote concerning the Lowering of Productivity"), published in 1963.

CHAPTER 4 ENDNOTES

1. To date, I have yet to meet a Spanish-speaker named Igor, but I shall remain vigilant.

CHAPTER 5 ENDNOTES

1. You can find the full text of the poem "Jabberwocky" here: www.poetryfoundation.org/poems-and-poets/poems/detail/42916.

2. Gabriel Wyner, *Fluent Forever: How to Learn Any Language Fast and Never Forget It*, New York, NY: Harmony Books, 2014.

CHAPTER 6 ENDNOTES

1. Mark Davies, *A Frequency Dictionary of Spanish*, New York, NY: Routledge Press, 2006.

CLOSING ENDNOTES

1. Joel Kotkin, *The Next Hundred Million: America in 2050*, New York, NY: Penguin Press, 2010.

2. Frederick C. Croxton, William P. Dillingham, *Statistical Review of Immigration, 1820–1910. Distribution of immigrants, 1850–1900 Presented by Mr. Dillingham*, Reports of the Immigration Committee, Washington Government Printing Office, 1911.

3. Bracero History Archive, *Bittersweet Harvest: The Bracero Program*. Accessed on March 17, 2017. http://braceroarchive.org/about. ⊠

4. Ibid.

5. Geoff Colvin, *Humans are Underrated*, New York, NY: Portfolio, 2015.

Index

W